NATHANIEL HAWTHORNE

A Study of the Short Fiction

Also available in Twayne's Studies in Short Fiction Series

Twayne's Studies in Short Fiction

Gordon Weaver, General Editor
Oklahoma State University

NATHANIEL HAWTHORNE, Portrait by Charles Osgood, 1840
Used by permission of Essex Institute

NATHANIEL HAWTHORNE

A *Study of the Short Fiction*

Nancy Bunge
Michigan State University

TWAYNE PUBLISHERS · *NEW YORK*
Maxwell Macmillan Canada · *Toronto*
Maxwell Macmillan International · *New York Oxford Singapore Sydney*

Twayne's Studies in Short Fiction Series, No. 41

Copyright © 1993 by Twayne Publishers

Twayne Publishers
Macmillan Publishing Company
866 Third Avenue
New York, New York 10022

Maxwell Macmillan Canada, Inc.
1200 Eglinton Avenue East
Suite 200
Don Mills, Ontario M3C 3N1

Library of Congress Cataloging-in-Publication Data

Bunge, Nancy L.
    Nathaniel Hawthorne : a study of the short fiction / Nancy Bunge.
       p.   cm. — (Twayne's studies in short fiction ; no. 41)
    Includes bibliographical references (p.   ) and index.
    ISBN 0-8057-0852-9
    1. Hawthorne, Nathaniel, 1804–1864—Criticism and interpretation
  2. Short story. I. Title. II. Series.
PS1888.B8   1993
813'.3—dc20   92-38700
                                                     CIP

10 9 8 7 6 5 4 3 2 1

Printed in the United States of America

Contents

Preface

When Melville dedicated *Moby Dick* to Nathaniel Hawthorne and Henry James wrote a book of criticism about him, they established Hawthorne's literary significance. Subsequent authors and scholars have not only certified these early recognitions, but as Hawthorne's interpreters learn more about history, literature, and psychology, they recognize new depths in his work.

In this book, I have attempted, above all, to help readers begin to explore the intellectual and emotional richness of Hawthorne's tales. Although I have learned much from other Hawthorne scholars, I have concentrated on Hawthorne's short fiction rather than on theories about it. In order to focus on the thirty-one tales and sketches I analyze, I indicate only general patterns of critical interpretation. I discuss the best-known stories along with a significant number of more obscure works, but had I an indulgent audience, I would also write about the other sixty-six tales and sketches. I have never read an uninteresting Hawthorne short story.

Herman Melville identified what makes Hawthorne's tales fascinating: the quality of mind and of heart permeating them. Again and again, Hawthorne's stories bring up unpleasant human traits with such compassion his readers not only look their worst selves in the face, they recognize themselves. The Hawthorne criticism I best recall came from a student who said that at first, Hawthorne's stories struck her as bizarre, but after thinking about them, she realized he'd written about her. I hope this book helps others reach the same conclusion, for Hawthorne's tales grow from a perspective so optimistic, it assumes that acknowledging rather than avoiding all aspects of themselves, even the worst, allows human beings to move from sentimentality to serenity.

The insight and kindness of many people have influenced this book. I hope and suspect twenty years of teaching students who insist I explain to them and to myself why literature matters have helped me to understand why Hawthorne's tales have moved so many readers. The Hawthorne criticism I have read over the past twenty-five years has undoubtedly sharpened my readings and improved the way I answer my students' questions. So I must also thank those multitudes of commentators who have helped me appreciate the complexity and depth of Hawthorne's short stories. I owe a particular debt to the three scholars who supervised my doctoral dissertation on Hawthorne's tales twenty years ago: the late Harry Hayden Clark, William T. Lenehan, and Merton M. Sealts, Jr. They would not necessarily agree with my analyses here, but the care and seriousness they brought to evaluating my work taught me to read closely, to listen carefully to others, and, finally, to trust my own reactions. As Harry Hayden Clark's teaching assistant, I often asked him for advice; he usually replied, "Use your own good judgment, Miss Bunge." I've tried to do that here. If I have successfully illuminated Hawthorne for others, the credit must go to those who did the same for me.

Thanks also to Melissa Solomon of Twayne Publishers for her help, efficiency, and enthusiasm. And I thank Gordon Weaver, the general editor of this series, for encouraging me, for giving me good advice, and for offering it so kindly I could hear it.

Acknowledgements

The quotations from Hawthorne's works in the text as well as the excerpts from his works and letters in "The Writer" are reprinted by permission from *The Scarlet Letter, The House of Seven Gables, Our Old Home, A Wonder Book and Tanglewood Tales, The American Notebooks, Twice-Told Tales, Mosses from an Old Manse, The Snow-Image and Uncollected Tales, The Letters 1813-1843, The Letters 1843-1853, The Letters 1853-1856, The Letters 1857-1864*, volumes I, II, V, VII, VIII, IX, X, XI, XV, XVI, XVII, and XVIII, respectively of *The Centenary Edition of the Works of Nathaniel Hawthorne*, 20 vols. edited by William Charvat, Roy Harvey Pearce, Claude M. Simpson, Fredson Bowers, Matthew J. Bruccoli, L. Neal Smith, John Manning, J. Donald Cowley, Thomas Woodson, Norman Holmes Pearson, Bill Ellis, James A. Rubino, James Kayes, copyright 1962, 1965, 1970, 1972, 1972, 1974, 1974, 1974, 1984, 1985, 1987, 1987, respectively, by the Ohio State University Press.

Excerpts from Herman Melville, *The Piazza Tales*, ed. Harrison Hayford, Alma A. MacDougall, G. Thomas Tanselle, et al. The Writings of Herman Melville, The Northwestern-Newberry Edition, Volume IX. Copyright 1987, Northwestern University Press and the Newberry Library, Evanston and Chicago. Reprinted by permission.

Excerpts from *Hawthorne's Fiction: The Light & the Dark*, by Richard Harter Fogle. Copyright © 1952 by the University of Oklahoma Press.

Excerpts from "Thwarted Nature: Nathaniel Hawthorne as Feminist" by Nina Baym. Reprinted with permission of G. K. Hall, an imprint of Macmillan Publishing Company from *American Novelists Revisited: Essays in Feminist Criticism*, edited by Fritz Fleischmann. Copyright © 1982 by Fritz Fleischmann.

Excerpts from *The Province of Piety: Moral History in Hawthorne's Early Tales* by Michael J. Colacurcio reprinted by permission of the publishers, Cambridge, Mass.: Harvard University Press, copyright 1984 by the President and Fellows of Harvard College.

Excerpts from *Family Themes and Hawthorne's Fiction* by Gloria Ehrlich. Copyright © 1984 by Rutgers, The State University.

Part 1

THE SHORT FICTION

The philosophical ruminations persistently accompanying and interpreting the events in Nathaniel Hawthorne's fiction invite the false impression he wrote essays disguised as stories. That these tales frequently conclude with a moral seems to confirm Hawthorne's characters exist solely to illustrate a thesis. Hawthorne encourages this misunderstanding, as in his introduction to "Rappaccini's Daughter," where he poses as a French critic and appraises his work: "His writings . . . might have won him greater reputation but for an inveterate love of allegory, which is apt to invest his plots and characters with the aspect of scenery and people in the clouds, and to steal away the human warmth out of his conceptions" (10:91–92).[1] Despite his self-deprecating judgments, the otherworldly quality of Hawthorne's tales reflects, not an inability to accommodate feeling, but a broad, inclusive point of view. Even Hawthorne's penchant for self-criticism reveals his determination to assess his writing as unblinkingly as he urges his readers to question their stereotypes, their behavior, and their society. To accomplish this, he conjures up a fictional world both recalling and transcending the commonplace.

When Hawthorne writes about battles rich with historic significance, for instance, he eschews ideology, including patriotism and pacifism. Hawthorne acknowledges some wars have justification, war does enormous damage, and, above all, the limits of human knowledge make any one judgment of any one war incomplete. In "Chiefly about War Matters," Hawthorne notes poor Southerners will benefit most from a Northern victory, "for thence would come the regeneration of a people—the removal of a foul scurf that has overgrown their life, and keeps them in a state of disease and decrepitude, one of the chief symptoms of which is, that, the more they suffer and are debased, the more they imagine themselves strong and beautiful." Hawthorne does not find this irony startling, for, despite their best efforts to believe otherwise, people wander through a world far beyond their understanding and control: "No human effort, on a grand scale, has ever yet resulted accordingly to the purpose of its projectors. The advantages are always incidental. Man's accidents are God's purposes. We miss the good we sought, and do the good we little cared for."[2]

Despite their ignorance, people must choose. Someone drafted for a war must weigh its value and make the best possible decision, for lives depend on it. But in the imagination one can explore possibilities and complications without considering consequences. Hawthorne's work gives the impression of unreality because it encourages a complex perspective incompatible with the resolution that produces action. And later, when his readers must again act, Hawthorne's "airy" ruminations may enrich their understanding and improve their choices.

Rather than grounding his tales with realistic descriptions of characters and events, Hawthorne relies heavily on concrete particulars his tales elevate into symbols, provoking his readers to respond to and understand familiar experiences in extraordinary ways. Instead of reinforcing quotidian awareness, Hawthorne's images speak from and to the unconscious that people dream their way into every night and set aside when they rise from their beds to act. In Hawthorne's tale "The Birthmark," the narrator contends dreams expose something truer than what most consider reality: "Truth often finds its way to the mind close-muffled in robes of sleep, and then speaks with uncompromising directness of matters in regard to which we practise an unconscious self-deception, during our waking moments" (10:40). One might make the same argument about Hawthorne's tales.

Not content with evoking the unconscious background of decisions, Hawthorne also examines the Puritan roots of American civilization. Hawthorne's explorations of the psychological dynamics at work in Puritan society give the saying "those who do not remember the past are condemned to repeat it" a post-Freudian significance. Hawthorne knew his contemporaries would hang no witches, but they undoubtedly saw "evil" in others they did not want to own in themselves. Most human beings preserve and use the arrogance that killed the Salem witches. Wars and revolutions cannot remove this curse; only humility and awareness can alleviate it. By exposing the lethal consequences of prejudice in people connected to, yet removed from, themselves, Hawthorne helps his audience lower their defenses enough to recognize and reflect on the frailties turning people against each other instead of binding them together. So Hawthorne's use of history, like the contemplative stance of his tales, helps his readers set aside practical concerns to reflect on their lives and their history.

The Puritans provide a natural subject for Hawthorne since they embody the self-righteous he sees as the antithesis of wisdom. Our national sense of ancestry begins with the Declaration of Independence's celebration of equality, reason, and individual freedom. Hawthorne recalls our nation's earlier, less attractive founding fathers who embraced hierarchy, revelation, and authoritarianism. Hawthorne's insistence on bringing up the irrational, bigoted dimension of our history reflects his habit of bringing to awareness reality's most discomforting elements. He complicates the issue further by not only acknowledging Puritan strengths, but also showing how they collaborate with Puritan shortcomings. Slavish obedience to a divinely inspired community allowed the Puritans to rejoice in the destruction of witches, to burn Indians for the glory of God, and to lay the foundations for democracy on a patch of rocky land in New England. Hawthorne's fictions acknowledge all of this.

If Hawthorne could hear the critics debate the meaning, not only of the whole body of his work, but of each tale, he would probably smile at his success. He could achieve no higher goal than to provoke discussion between alternative perspectives, except perhaps to encourage the realization that human limits push people to strive for as much understanding as possible while placing truth permanently beyond their grasp. Hawthorne identifies "adding wisdom to wisdom, throughout Eternity"[3] as the activity distinguishing human beings from animals. And he suggests that admitting ignorance and ameliorating it by multiplying perspectives brings joy as well as insight, for "every . . . view from a different position, creates a surprise in the mind" (8:104). Not only does the process of learning delight, Hawthorne believes the most rewarding human activity, love, rests on and grows from this ability to acknowledge different points of view.

Since Hawthorne enjoyed looking at reality from various angles, the short story seems his natural genre; writing tales allows him to explore a throng of awarenesses. The relatively short length facilitates readers' entry into the extraordinary worlds and characters Hawthorne sets loose. Few could tolerate an entire novel about a creature built of snow, but "The Snow-Image" makes a moving short story. Themes, characters, and techniques first developed in the tales resurface in Hawthorne's novels, but the novels in no way replicate the intellectual, emotional, and aesthetic range of Hawthorne's short fiction.

Hawthorne even complicates point of view within each story. The concluding morals convince most readers to appropriate them and confidently move on to the next tale. But Hawthorne warns at the start of *The House of the Seven Gables* that fiction built on a clear thesis has little value: "The Author has considered it hardly worth his while, therefore, relentlessly to impale the story with its moral, as with an iron rod" (2:2). This statement makes all Hawthorne's homilies suspect, a cynicism usually rewarded and reinforced by close examination of all the components at work in his tales and novels. Hawthorne's morals make careful readers uneasy, forcing them to repeatedly rethink and reanalyze both his fiction and the issues it raises. The tales with unreliable narrators make no sense until readers supply them with meaningful structures.

In the "Custom-House" section of *The Scarlet Letter*, Hawthorne describes himself as "a man who felt it to be the best definition of happiness to live throughout the whole range of his faculties and sensibilities" (1:40). His novels confirm the truth of this statement, but his short stories certify it. Hawthorne valued complexity so profoundly, and the body of his short fiction embodies it so tellingly, it seems appropriate to make their broadmindedness central to this analysis of them. So this chapter will discuss his short stories according to subject areas, emphasizing the diverse viewpoints offered on each topic.

Isolation and Community

Since even the most cursory review of Hawthorne's life and work unearths a variety of warnings against isolation, critics and teachers fall naturally into describing Hawthorne's work as a celebration of community. On its face, this characterization seems accurate. Hawthorne's letters and notebooks testify to his joy at abandoning solitude to become a deliriously happy husband and father. But Hawthorne enjoyed normalcy more in theory than in practice. While he remained consistently devoted to his family, holding down a regular job did not improve his writing as he had hoped. Although he anticipated ordinary work would give him deeper insight and enrich his fiction, whenever he took a job, his writing stopped—even during his stay at Brook Farm, a community established, in part, to free its inhabitants for creative work. Intellectual freedom, not time, was the issue. The man who guessed that if he had retained his Custom House job, he would "make the dinner-hour the nucleus of the day, and . . . spend the rest of it, as an old dog spends it, asleep in the sunshine or shade" (1:40) considers ordinary life potentially lethal, a judgment confirmed by Hawthorne's job experience.

"My Kinsman, Major Molineux"

Hawthorne's "My Kinsman, Major Molineux" helps explain his suspicion of convention. In this story, Robin Molineux, a naive country boy, comes to the city in search of the successful uncle he hopes will help him rise in the world. But when he asks where his uncle lives, people react mysteriously. These encounters establish the disjunction between the country world Robin has left and the cosmopolitan one he hopes to enter. For instance, Robin repeatedly runs into a distinguished-looking gentleman whose appearance contrasts with Robin's point-by-point. While Robin sports a "three-cornered hat, which in its better days had perhaps sheltered the graver bow of the lad's father," the man wears a "full periwig of grey hair." The boy has a "coarse grey coat, well worn, but in excellent repair," while the old man dresses in more elegant "wide-skirted coat of dark cloth." Robin's blue woolen stockings are "the incontrovertible handiwork of a mother or a sister"; the man has "silk stockings rolled about his knees." Robin walks with "a heavy cudgel, formed of an oak sapling, and retaining a part of the hardened root," while the man carries "a long and polished cane." These descriptions contrast Robin's naturalness and with the man's civility, an impression reinforced when Robin asks directions:

> The citizen . . . turned a long favored countenance upon Robin, and answered him in a tone of excessive anger and annoyance. His two sepulchral hems, however, broke into the very center of his rebuke, with the most singular effect, like a thought of the cold grave obtruding among wrathful passions.
> "Let go of my garment, fellow! I tell you, I know not the man you speak of. What! I have authority, I have—hem, hem—authority; and if this be the respect you show your betters, your feet shall be brought acquainted with the stocks, by daylight, tomorrow morning!" (11:209–211)

This cultured man threatens Robin with socially approved punishment; Robin considers responding more directly: "'The man is old, or verily—I might be tempted to turn back and smite him on the nose'" (11:211).

When Robin asks directions at an inn, the host notes his resemblance to the boy described on a wanted poster. Again, Robin thinks about using his cudgel and, again, restrains himself. Time after time, Robin meets irrational hostility expressed through threats to use the law against him. And, time after time, he suppresses his anger and rationalizes this unkindness, whenever possible invoking jealousy of his uncle's status.

Robin meets one very friendly person: a woman wearing a red petticoat who promises to take him to his uncle. He doubts her word, but she attracts him: "Though Robin read in her eyes what he did not hear in her words, yet the slender waisted woman, in the scarlet petticoat, proved stronger than the athletic country youth" (11:218). Robin manages to resist her, just barely. So Robin experiences human irrationality from within himself as well as from others.

The depth of Robin's need to believe the world rational becomes clear when he sees a man with a red and black face: "A few moments were consumed in philosophical speculations, upon the species of the *genus homo*, who had just left him, but having settled this point shrewdly, rationally, and satisfactorily, he was compelled to look elsewhere for amusement" (11:220–221). Surely someone capable of producing a shrewd, rational, and satisfactory explanation for a red and black face has more interest in constructing a logical scheme for his experience than in facing reality. Robin needs to prove people reasonable; if society does not function sensibly, how can he endure it, let alone rise in it?

As Robin rests from his intellectual labors, an awareness of human cruelty touches him. Studying the moonlight on a church, he muses, "Was that heavenly light the visible sanctity of the place, visible because no earthly and impure feet were within the walls?" This fleeting recognition of human evil makes "Robin's heart shiver with a sensation of loneliness, stronger than he had ever felt in the remotest depths of his native woods" (11:222).

So, in fantasy, Robin retreats to those woods and its sweet community. The life he has just abandoned, now attracts him; its order comforts him: "There, at the going down of the summer sun, it was his father's custom to perform domestic worship, that the neighbors might come and join with him like brothers of the family, and that the wayfaring man might pause to drink at that fountain, and keep his heart pure by freshening the memory of home" (11:222). But reality contaminates these memories, for even in his fantasies, all his family members feel sad about Robin's departure, but only the youngest expresses it. Just beneath the pastoral contentment lies a grief expressed only by the one too small to know how to behave: "He perceived the slight inequality of his father's voice when he came to speak of the Absent One; he noted how his mother turned her face to the broad and knotted trunk; how his elder brother scorned, because the beard was rough upon his upper lip, to permit his features to be moved; how the younger sister drew down a low hanging branch before her eyes; and how the little one of all, whose sports had hitherto broken the decorum of the scene, understood the prayer for her playmate, and burst into clamorous grief" (11:223). Social codes distort even the honesty of life at home.

Eventually, a kind man stops and tells Robin that if he waits, his uncle will appear. As the man promises, a procession materializes with his uncle, the British representative, tarred and feathered. Here, Hawthorne presents a moment in the American Revolution through the eyes of a hurt, disappointed boy. Hawthorne's portrait of the revolutionaries contains little patriotic pride: "On they went, like fiends that throng in mockery round some dead potentate, mighty no more, but majestic still in his agony. On they went, in counterfeited pomp, in senseless uproar, in frenzied merriment, trampling all on an old man's heart" (11:230).

The scene is nightmarish. The townspeople Robin encountered earlier reconvene in disarray. The distinguished gentleman resurfaces in his nightgown: "In front of the Gothic window stood the old citizen, wrapped in a wide gown, his gray periwig exchanged for a nightcap, which was thrust back from his forehead, and his silk stockings hanging down about his legs. He supported himself on his polished cane in a fit of convulsive merriment, which manifested itself on his solemn old features, like a funny inscription on a tomb-stone." Robin feels "a sort of mental inebriety" (11:229–230) the tale's hallucinated images communicate to the readers.

By making the scene dreamlike, Hawthorne captures the natural reaction of a young boy first recognizing cruelty. And by piling up absurd, incomplete, disjointed images of supposedly civilized people acting like lunatics, Hawthorne helps the reader understand along with Robin what ugliness lurks behind cultural facades. Knowledge of human cruelty hurts at all ages, but it strikes innocence with particular vehemence. If the kind gentleman did not stand beside him, Robin probably could not bear to watch.

This harsh characterization of the crowd coordinates with the tale's opening, where the narrator explains the colonists' unfair reactions to their British representatives: "The people looked with most jealous scrutiny to the exercise of power, which did not emanate from themselves, and they usually rewarded the rulers with slender gratitude, for the compliances, by which, in softening their instructions from beyond the sea, they had incurred the reprehension of those who gave them" (11:208). Correspondingly, the procession seems not a realization of reason and freedom, but an outpouring of meanness and absurdity, appropriately led by the man with the red and black face who "appeared like war personified; the red of one cheek was an emblem of fire and sword; the blackness of the other betokened the mourning which attends them" (11:227). Order breaks down; all are "demanding the explanation, which not a soul could give" (11:227). The world rocks with cruel laughter.

Robin joins in: "The contagion was spreading among the multitude, when, all at once, it seized upon Robin, and he sent forth a shout of laughter that echoed through the street; every man shook his sides, every man emptied his lungs, but Robin's shout was the loudest there" (11:230). Robin's participation shows the link between the apparent joy of these revolutionaries and the despair undergirding and feeding all sadism, even that given political justification.

When Robin understands that the rational society he hoped to join does not exist, he wants to go home. But the gentleman who has stood by him and who earlier suggested to Robin that "one man [may] have several voices" (11:226) urges him to wait a few days. Perhaps Robin will even decide to stay permanently: "If you prefer to remain with us, perhaps, as you are a shrewd youth, you may rise in the world, without the help of your kinsman, Major Molineux" (11:231). Just as the gentleman encouraged Robin to face his uncle, he now coaxes Robin toward acceptance of human absurdity. Despite Robin's fantasies of escape to a place populated by kind, religious relatives, once he has tasted the irrationality of both himself and others, he cannot return to innocence. He must learn to live with his new awareness. And as long as honest, kind people stand by his side, he may be able to do so.

The reader closes the tale hoping, along with the gentleman, that Robin will put his insight to constructive use. Although Robin's disillusionment hurts him, taking on society without realizing its institutions reflect human irrationality would leave Robin permanently lost, following one misleading set of instructions after another.

This reading of "My Kinsman, Major Molineux" seems compatible with most critical analyses. The different readings reflect primarily the diverse external materials critics bring to bear on this story. The most popular approaches to the story are historical and psychological. Psychoanalytic critics, like Frederick Crews, define Robin's growth in terms of his shifting relationships to various father-figures. Other critics, like Roy Harvey Pearce, put the tale in the context of the American Revolution, a number of them seeing the story as challenging the philosophy articulated in Ben Franklin's *Autobiography*. Other critics, like Terence Martin, fuse these two notions, declaring this a tale about individual and national maturity. As Robert Penn Warren remarks, the true miracle of the story is its ability to sustain so many approaches: "We are not dealing with the standard type of allegory but with a pervasive and massive symbolism, the basic symbol being the story itself which, in its literalism, absorbs and fuses the various kinds of import."[4] "My Kinsman, Major Molineux" provides a particularly strong example of the value of Hawthorne's critics as well as the futility of debating who has the correct answer. The richness of Hawthorne's tales allows them to absorb a multitude of aesthetic, religious, historical, and psychological explanations.

"Young Goodman Brown"

Hawthorne's Puritan tales explain more fully the dynamics behind the collective delirium described in "My Kinsman, Major Molineux," as well as the consequences of not recognizing the irrational component of convention. Those who prize community could not find a more troubling element of our national history than the reign of these fanatical, but loyal ancestors; Hawthorne's fiction acknowledges this difficulty. And he did not write out of ignorant fantasies about the Puritans. "Young Goodman Brown" not only presents the issue of the Salem witch trials, but a number of its characters have the names of Salem residents charged with witchcraft, and its major action takes place in the noisy pasture historical documents of the period designate as a witches' gathering place. Hawthorne does not simply provide a record of the time, he uses history to examine issues of community and individualism explaining both the madness in Salem and much subsequent madness.

Ostensibly, this tale indicts arrogant individualism. Young Goodman Brown, either in dream or in fact, almost joins a witches' sabbath in the forest. He turns away at the last moment because he does not want to confess his evil. Ironically, his exemplary behavior produces a life of isolation and gloom: "A stern, a sad, a darkly meditative, a distrustful, if not a desperate man, did he become, from the night of that fearful dream" (10:89). He despises his townspeople because he believes they participated in the evil ceremony he resisted. He sees nothing but their sinfulness. His wife, Faith, particularly offends him: "Often, awakening suddenly at midnight, he shrank from the bosom of Faith, and at morning or eventide, when the family knelt down at prayer, he scowled, and muttered to himself, and gazed sternly at his wife, and turned away" (10:89). Brown has a classic case of projection. Unable to deal with his own frailty, he sees and hates it in everyone else. So the tale seems to celebrate humility.

But Brown learns complacency from his community. He lives in a society that ruthlessly judges evil in everyone else. He resists the demonic figure who urges him towards the witches' sabbath because he suspects that acting out his sinful impulses will bring dishonor on his family. The devil laughs at Brown's innocence: "I have been as well acquainted with your family as with ever a one among the Puritans; and that's no trifle to say. I helped your grandfather, the constable, when he lashed the Quaker woman so smartly through the streets of Salem. And it was I that brought your father a pitch-pine knot, kindled at my own hearth, to set fire to an Indian village, in King Philip's war" (10:77). In other words, Puritan "goodness" has justified gross violations of people the Puritans perceived as bad, such as Quakers and Native Americans. Brown's decision to declare himself good and assign all the evil to others has strong community history.

The tale also calls into question the quality of Brown's present social and family life since Brown functions as a beloved father and prized citizen, even though he despises everyone: "He had lived long, and was borne to his grave, a hoary corpse, followed by Faith, an aged woman, and children and grandchildren, a goodly procession, besides neighbors, not a few" (10:89–90).

So, although this tale condemns arrogance and recommends community, it acknowledges the difficulties of distinguishing real and apparent solidarity. People long to belong and they almost inevitably attempt to win acceptance by following socially approved patterns. But this faith in their family, society, or nation assumes that convention grows from wisdom, not habit. Those willing to resist society's self-righteousness may achieve the humility necessary to genuine fellowship, but they will have trouble making themselves understood. On the other hand, the community will support those who ask no questions. Societies encourage conformity because the assumption that this state, unlike all others, rests on a bedrock of truth, cannot survive examination. So behavior deviating from this complacency needs speedy and forceful correction.

No one understood the social value of brute authoritarianism better than the Puritans. Following group norms does guarantee people a place to belong; since this unity rests on compliance rather than reflection and choice, it is collective illusion. Mindlessly following community rules turns human beings into robots, and robots cannot love, but they rarely notice their isolation because robots cannot think either.

Brown and the other members of his society suppress their emotional lives because they suspect, correctly, that if they loosen the reins on their passions, they may discover "sinful" feelings at odds with divine wisdom as defined by their ministers.

Hawthorne emphasizes the split between convention and the unconscious by having Brown move from the town to the country as he follows his impulses. The deeper he moves into the forest, the more completely he becomes one with his "evil." At the center of the woods stands a collection of respectable people whose presence confesses their secret sins:

> Either the sudden gleams of light, flashing over the obscure field, bedazzled Goodman Brown, or he recognized a score of the church-members of Salem village, famous for their especial sanctity. Good old Deacon Gookin had arrived, and waited at the skirts of that venerable saint, his revered pastor. But, irreverently consorting with these grave, reputable, and pious people, these elders of the church, these chaste dames and dewy virgins, there were men of dissolute lives and women of spotted fame, wretches given over to all mean and filthy vice, and suspected even of horrid crimes. It was strange to see, that the good shrank not from the wicked, nor were the sinners abashed by the saints. (10:85)

The dreamlike atmosphere of the scene as well as the frame Hawthorne puts around the tale suggesting Brown may have dreamt the episode, link the witches' sabbath to the unconscious. Since the ability to suppress socially unacceptable impulses helps determine social standing, in the realm of the unconscious, people do enjoy relative equality.

Brown's resistance to evil seems natural, but the tale ties sinfulness to nature: "Verse after verse was sung, and still the chorus of the desert swelled between, like the deepest tone of mighty organ. And, with the final peal of that dreadful anthem, there came a sound, as if the roaring wind, the rushing streams, the howling beasts, and every other voice of the unconverted wilderness, were mingling and according with the voice of guilty man, in homage to the prince of all" (10:85–86). The demonic figure conducting the witches' sabbath makes explicit the link between sin and humanity: "Evil is the nature of mankind. Evil must be your only happiness. Welcome, again, my children, to the communion of your race!" (10:88).

Compassionately accepting human frailty could indeed help the Puritans build genuine community. All people *are* sinful and can connect with each other honestly and directly only after facing and confessing this aspect of themselves. But Brown turns away from this insight, lives in terms of social codes, and destroys his life by attempting to preserve his goodness. The tale presents this truth so starkly that, despite the enormous volume of critical commentary on this story, most acknowledge it as the tale's theme. It seems appropriate so many scholars have brought so much attention to this story, since it powerfully evokes one of Hawthorne's central ideas: the destructive consequences of ignoring the disjunction between universal frailty and societal arrogance.

"Roger Malvin's Burial"

"Roger Malvin's Burial" shows that violating one's heart to obey convention can hurt others as well as oneself. Stranded in the woods with his mortally wounded future father-in-law, Roger Malvin, Reuben Bourne must decide whether to stay and perish with Roger or try to save himself by leaving. His father-in-law urges him to go, but asks Roger to return and bury his corpse. The narrator explains this request: "An almost superstitious regard . . . was paid by the frontier inhabitants to the rites of sepulture; and there are many instances of the sacrifice of life, in the attempt to bury those who had fallen by the 'sword of the wilderness'" (10:344–345). Roger promises and leaves, although reluctantly, because he wants to live: "His generous nature would fain have delayed him, at whatever risk, till the dying scene were past; but the desire of existence, and the hope of happiness had strengthened in his heart, and he was unable to resist them" (10:345).

When Roger returns home, he tells his future wife, Dorcas, of her father's death. She immediately asks if he buried her father. The narrator describes this as "the question by which her filial piety manifested itself" (10:348); Dorcas automatically translates feelings into group norms. Reuben fears losing her if he tells the truth, so he says: "My hands were weak, but I did what I could. . . . There stands a noble tomb-stone above his head, and I would to Heaven I slept as soundly as he!" (10:348). Then Reuben begins to feel guilty, not for leaving Roger, but because "concealment had imparted to a justifiable act, much of the secret effect of guilt" (10:349).

Although Reuben's dishonesty preserves his relationship to Dorcas and his stature in the community, guilt destroys his life. Miserable with himself, he behaves miserably to others. He loves only his son, Cyrus, "as if whatever was good and happy in his own nature had been transferred to his child, carrying his affections with it" (10:351). When bankruptcy drives him from town, he sets out with Dorcas and Cyrus. As they travel to a new life, Reuben strays from his route; his guilt unconsciously pulls him to the place he left Roger Malvin. Reuben accepts this diversion because "he trusted that it was Heaven's intent to afford him an opportunity of expiating his sin" (10:356).

As they journey through the woods, Reuben hears a noise, shoots, and discovers that he has killed his son in the same place he left Roger Malvin to die. When Dorcas investigates the noise, Reuben confesses the truth to her. At that moment, he becomes, once more, a feeling human being: "Then Reuben's heart was stricken, and the tears gushed out like water from a rock" (10:360). Reuben can now pray: "The vow that the wounded youth had made, the blighted man had come to redeem. His sin was expiated, the curse was gone from him; and, in the hour, when he had shed blood dearer to him than his own, a prayer, the first for years, went up to Heaven from the lips of Reuben Bourne" (10:360). Some critics accept the narrator's apparent judgment here: Reuben redeems his life by killing his son. Others proclaim Reuben's salvation a psychological delusion, offering diverse explanations of his error. The view of the second group seems more consistent with the whole tale.

Reuben's peace costs too much. He has ruined his life and killed his son because of guilt over violating a superstition. The story's enigmatic historical introduction reinforces the notion that Reuben's relief comes at too dear a price. As the tale opens, the narrator explains that Roger and Reuben had fought in "Lovell's Flight," a battle conducted "in accordance with civilized ideas of valor." But the narrator seems ambivalent about this bravery: "*Imagination, by casting certain circumstances judiciously into the shade,* may see much to admire in the heroism of a little band, who gave battle to twice their number." Later, the narrator indicates what complications prevent him from venerating this conflict: "The battle, *though so fatal to those who fought,* was not unfortunate in its consequences to the country; for it broke the strength of a tribe, and conduced to the peace which subsisted during several ensuing years" (10:337; italics mine). Sacrificing lives for a few years' peace does not seem wise. Similarly, killing his son brings Reuben peace from pointless guilt, but had he the courage to confess violating a cultural superstition in the first place, he could have avoided both the death of his son and a destructive, emotionally arid life.

Ironically, Reuben's lie kills not only his child, but also the relationship it protected. He could not tell Dorcas the truth for fear of losing her, but that same untruth puts a rift between them: "Even Dorcas, though loving and beloved, was far less dear to him; for Reuben's secret thoughts and insulated emotions had gradually made him a selfish man; and he could no longer love deeply, except where he saw, or imagined, some reflection or likeness of his own mind" (10:351). But Dorcas fails to notice.

Since hearing of her father's death makes Dorcas wonder, first and foremost, if her fiancé gave him a proper burial, it is not surprising she overlooks Reuben's coolness. Dorcas consistently substitutes convention for emotional truths. As her son and husband approach the denouement of their fatal drama, she comforts herself with a sentimental ballad: "As Dorcas sang, the walls of her forsaken home seemed to encircle her; she no longer saw the gloomy pines, nor heard the wind, which still, as she began each verse, sent a heavy breath through the branches, and died away in a hollow moan, from the burthen of the song" (10:358). Dorcas's comforting stereotypes help destroy her son and her husband.

This tale, like "Young Goodman Brown," uses movement from town to forest to symbolize the shift from conscious to unconscious awareness. The woods in "Young Goodman Brown" have a darkness and mystery that complement the witches' ceremony, while the forest in "Roger Malvin's Burial" bursts with sunlight until the final tragedy. As Dorcas sings to herself, "the sunshine yet lingered upon the higher branches of the trees that grew on rising ground; but the shades of evening had deepened into the hollow, where the encampment was made" (10:357). All corruption in the woods comes from human beings following social codes. The tree Reuben tied with a cloth to identify the place he left Roger Malvin flourishes except that "A blight had apparently stricken the upper part of the oak, and the very topmost bough was withered, sapless, and utterly dead. Reuben remembered how the little banner had fluttered on the topmost bough, when it was green and lovely, eighteen years before. Whose guilt had blasted it?" (10:357). Although "Young Goodman Brown" and "Roger Malvin's Burial" use the contrast between the forest and the town differently, in both tales this imagery shows how suppressing natural frailty to accommodate social norms ruins people's lives.

"Lady Eleanore's Mantle"

Lady Eleanore of "Lady Eleanore's Mantle" also pays for putting her natural impulses aside to satisfy community standards. A representative of European aristocracy, Lady Eleanore wears an elaborately embroidered mantle that reminds the democratic Americans among whom she lives of her superior background. When she catches the smallpox, rumor associates the mantle with her illness. Lady Eleanore herself makes the connection when she attributes the disease to her conceit: "'The curse of Heaven hath stricken me, because I would not call man my brother, nor woman sister. I wrapped myself in PRIDE as in a MANTLE, and scorned the sympathies of nature; and therefore has nature made this wretched body the medium of a dreadful sympathy'" (9:287). Most critics agree with Lady Eleanore's self-condemnation. Lady Eleanore, like Young Goodman Brown and Reuben Bourne, seems the victim of cultural arrogance.

While the other tales indict vague social standards, this story directly implicates Lady Eleanore's contemporaries in her pride, as noted by a minority of the tale's commentators.[5] Democrats, ostensibly opposed to the aristocratic leanings she represents, applaud and admire Lady Eleanore's beauty. Her most enthusiastic admirer, a young man named Jervase Helwyse, "a youth of no birth or fortune, or other advantages, save the mind and soul that nature gave him;" throws himself in front of her when Eleanore arrives, and the entire crowd of so-called democrats applauds when she steps on him: "Never, surely, was there an apter emblem of aristocracy and hereditary pride, trampling on human sympathies and the kindred of nature, than these two figures presented at that moment. Yet the spectators were so smitten with her beauty, and so essential did pride seem to the existence of such a creature, that they gave a simultaneous acclamation of applause" (9:276). The crowd could not encourage Lady Eleanore's conceit if they did not share it. Indeed, Lady Eleanore behaves cruelly for her audience at least as much as for herself.

When Helwyse approaches her at a ball attended by people almost as ridiculously dressed as herself, she sends him away, but confesses that if she listened to herself, she would not: "'Take him out of my sight if such be your pleasure; for I can find in my heart to do nothing but laugh at him—whereas, in all decency and conscience, it would become me to weep for the mischief I have wrought!'" (9:280). Lady Eleanore has wandered into a society of newly minted democrats who retain their aristocratic longings. She acts out for them the arrogance they pretend to have transcended.

When Providence apparently punishes Lady Eleanore for her vanity by infecting her with smallpox, it delights her admirers. She not only manifests their pride for them, she pays for it. Her illness pleases no one more than Jervase: "The malice of his mental disease, the bitterness lurking at the bottom of his heart, mad as he was, for a blighted and ruined life, and love that had been paid with cruel scorn, awoke within the breast of Jervase Helwyse. He shook his finger at the wretched girl, and the chamber echoed, the curtains of the bed were shaken, with his outburst of insane merriment" (9:287). The disease infects all levels of society, not solely the aristocracy.

Lady Eleanore's confession and her harsh self-criticism also show that all human beings, no matter how alienating their social norms, retain consciences. One can remove a mantle of arrogance, but that means having the courage to accept and act on one's humane instincts even though the world pushes one to violate them. Young Goodman Brown, Reuben Bourne, and Lady Eleanore come from and move through societies with different standards, but their inability to own and to act in terms of their own needs and impulses destroys them all. "Lady Eleanore's Mantle" seems the most pessimistic tale of the three because it implicates society most directly and takes place in an ostensibly democratic culture; it also offers the most hope, for Eleanore's feelings push her toward salvation. She repeatedly fights her empathy to conform.

"The Minister's Black Veil"

Although Young Goodman Brown, Reuben Bourne, and Lady Eleanore err in not owning their flaws, those who become obsessed with their evil also make a grave mistake. Hawthorne wants people to admit their frailty compassionately, not as an exercise in self-hate. In "The Minister's Black Veil," the Reverend Mr. Hooper startles his congregation by appearing for Sunday services with a black piece of cloth over his face. He wears the veil for the rest of his life, refusing to remove it even on his deathbed. He protests he must display this symbol of his evil to serve as a moral example: "What, but the mystery which it obscurely typifies, has made this piece of crape so awful? When the friend shows his inmost heart to his friend; the lover to his best-beloved; when man does not vainly shrink from the eye of his Creator, loathsomely treasuring up the secret of his sin; then deem me a monster, for the symbol beneath which I have lived, and die! I look around me, and, lo! on every visage a Black Veil!" (9:52).

Hooper's veil does educate. Others respond powerfully to him because it forces them to confront their depravity: "Each member of the congregation, the most innocent girl, and the man of hardened breast, felt as if the preacher had crept upon them, behind his awful veil, and discovered their hoarded iniquity of deed or thought. . . . An unsought pathos came hand in hand with awe" (9:40). While most attempt to evade this awareness, the dying realize they must face it and call for the Reverend Mr. Hooper. The veil also improves Hooper's funeral sermons: "It was a tender and heart-dissolving prayer, full of sorrow, yet so imbued with celestial hopes, that the music of a heavenly harp, swept by the fingers of the dead, seemed faintly to be heard among the saddest accents of the minister" (9:42). And, it ties him to the dead; one parishioner claims it makes him "ghost-like," (9:41) and at the end of his career, "he had one congregation in the church, and a more crowded one in the church-yard" (9:50). Because of the veil's positive consequences, many critics believe the tale validates Hooper's behavior.

But Hooper's parishioners disagree. They no longer welcome the minister at weddings or Sunday dinner. They believe some occasions go more smoothly without a living parable of evil present. People sin, but they also experience joy and love. By turning himself into an unrelenting example of depravity, Hooper demonstrates a lack of generosity, most of all toward himself. His veil shuts out happiness, giving "a darkened aspect to all living and inanimate things" (9:38). It may even distort his religious views, for it "threw its obscurity between him and the holy page, as he read the Scriptures" (9:39). A number of critics embrace this view of Hooper. Nor surprisingly, a third critical contingent, the smallest, argues that Hooper, like most human beings, is both noble and foolish.

Hooper's fiancée, Elizabeth, sides with this group of commentators. When she threatens to leave Hooper if he does not remove the veil, he begs her not to abandon him: "'Oh! you know not how lonely I am, and how frightened to be alone behind my black veil. Do not leave me in this miserable obscurity for ever!'" (9:47). Indeed, it does isolate him: "Thus, from beneath the black veil, there rolled a cloud into the sunshine, an ambiguity of sin or sorrow, which enveloped the poor minister, so that love or sympathy could never reach him" (9:48). But Elizabeth never leaves him. She sits at his deathbed, protecting the veil because it matters to him and because she loves him: "There was the nurse, no hired handmaiden of death, but one whose calm affection had endured thus long, in secresy, in solitude, amid the chill of age, and would not perish, even at the dying hour" (9:50). Love is there for Hooper, but the veil prevents him from seeing or enjoying it.

Hooper's veil operates just as destructively on its wearer as Lady Eleanore's mantle; Hooper's identification with his loathsomeness ruins his life as surely as Lady Eleanore's claim of superiority destroys hers. Nor does it matter that Lady Eleanore's contemporaries encourage her, while most of Hooper's signal their discomfort with his veil. The core issue rests deeper than whether one sees oneself as good or evil or whether one resists or conforms to community codes. Both tales affirm a compassion for oneself and others that grows from tolerating imperfection.

One genuine heroine emerges: Hooper's fiancée, Elizabeth. She does not approve of his action, she does not embrace his philosophy, but she also does not reject him for it. She loves him, so she supports him, even when he blunders. Unfortunately, Hooper, Bourne, Brown, and Lady Eleanore fail to achieve this balanced understanding of human error.

"The Man of Adamant"

"The Man of Adamant" counters any fantasies that trusting oneself means shutting out the world. The central character of this tale, Richard Digby, rejects Puritan society. He condemns the norms Reuben Bourne and Young Goodman Brown give too much credence and turns to his own faith. And he certainly does not become lost in self-hate like the Reverend Mr. Hooper. In order to keep his wisdom unadulterated by the views of others, he retreats into the same wilderness Brown and Bourne flee: "As his creed was like no man's else, and being well pleased that Providence had entrusted him, alone of mortals, with the treasure of a true faith, Richard Digby determined to seclude himself to the sole and constant enjoyment of his happy fortune" (11:161).

So he crawls into a cave in the densest part of the forest, misreads the Bible to himself, prays to himself, and laughs to himself. And he behaves just as inappropriately as the characters who mistrusted themselves. His error is so clear virtually every critic commenting on the tale agrees. Some of them, like Mark Van Doren, condemn the tale as obvious.

Not only does Roger illustrate contrasting faults, but the difference between Roger and the other characters shapes the story's imagery as well. While Brown and Bourne fear destruction if they disavow the sunlit world of the village, Digby sees it as dangerous. He curses the meeting-house, "which he regarded as a temple of heathen idolatry." He expects the entire Puritan community to dissolve in fire once the only good person in it, namely himself, leaves: "But, as the sunshine continued to fall peacefully on the cottages and fields, and the husbandmen labored and children played, and as there were many tokens of present happiness, and nothing ominous of speedy judgment, he turned away, some-what disappointed" (11:162).

And while Dorcas's sweet joy as her husband kills her son seems misguided, so does Digby's bitterness; he focuses on the dark as unde-viatingly as she sees the sunshine: "The shadow had now grown so deep, where he was sitting, that he made continual mistakes in what he read, converting all that was gracious and merciful, to denunciations of vengeance and unutterable woe, on every created being but himself" (11:166).

To better enjoy the darkness, Digby retreats into a cave, swallowing the water dripping from the ceiling instead of venturing out into the light to sip from a nearby stream, a fatal mistake for one whose heart already has started to turn to stone. Mary Goffe, an Englishwoman, like Lady Eleanore, appears and urges him to drink fresh water and return to society with her. She promises that trusting her will save him: "I pray thee, by thy hope of Heaven, and as thou wouldst not dwell in this tomb forever, drink of this hallowed water, be it but a single drop! Then, make room for me by thy side, and let us read together one page of that blessed volume—and, lastly, kneel down with me and pray! Do this; and thy stony heart shall become softer than a babe's, and all be well" (11:167). Since Mary Goffe has in fact died, this may be her spirit, as the narrator suggests, but, more probably, she represents Richard Digby's uncon-scious realization that he needs human sympathy. In any case, the moment she gives up and leaves, his heart stops and Richard Digby turns completely to rock, becoming a "freak of nature."

Here, the tale reverses the images from "Roger Malvin's Burial," for Reuben Bourne's conformity turns him to stone; only after his confes-sion can he weep. Richard Digby's isolation calcifies him, and water is associated with returning to society. But both tales condemn exclusive reliance on either convention or individualism, suggesting that every person knows instinctively the inappropriateness of both extremes.

The narrator consistently alludes to Mary's spirituality, at one point guessing she may be "a dreamlike spirit, typifying pure Religion" (11:168). In the tales considered thus far, Hawthorne presents three kinds of religion, one dominated by repressive community codes like Puritanism, one based on rampant individualism like Richard Digby's religion, and a "Pure Religion" dominated by a charity and gentleness notably absent in the other varieties of religious experience Hawthorne describes. This generosity embraces both human sinfulness and human goodness, oneself and others. This kindliness not only produces religious charity, it facilitates a complicated and intelligent view of the world.

After Richard dies, the community spreads out to his retreat, and a century after his death, playing children discover the cave that became Richard's tomb. When their father and mother see Richard's corpse, they immediately bury it with rocks. Although everyone wants to forget about Richard, no one does; for generations, people avoid his burial place. This aversion suggests others share Richard's arrogance; they struggle to forget this side of themselves, but cannot. If they had Mary Goffe's generosity, they would not fear Richard. This ending ties together "The Man of Adamant" and those tales critical of conformity, for it shows that those who consider themselves superior to their communities and those convinced of their society's righteousness both suffer from intolerance. Conformity and individualism both undermine compassion. On the other hand, Mary Goffe and Hooper's fiancée, Elizabeth, so thoroughly accept themselves, they have grace left for others.

"Egotism; or, the Bosom Serpent"

Hawthorne's tale "Egotism; or, the Bosom Serpent" provides a synopsis of issues raised in the earlier tales, as its central character, Roderick Elliston, replicates, one by one, the mistakes of all the unhappy characters discussed thus far. Roderick's problems begin when he separates from his wife, Rosina, and becomes absorbed in his own pain. As his egotism grows, it begins to manifest itself physically, as did Richard Digby's emotional hardness in "The Man of Adamant." Roderick starts to resemble the snake he claims draws his attention inward by gnawing his stomach.

First, Roderick attempts to cure his diseased self-interest by withdrawing from others, as did Reuben Bourne. But when word of his snake gets out, he enjoys the distinction, just as Lady Eleanore took pride in her differentness. As Roderick circulates, he discovers he can see the snakes in the bosoms of others; like Young Goodman Brown, he becomes conscious of others' evil. And like the Reverend Mr. Hooper he issues reprimands, but while Hooper lectures about secret sin, Roderick makes specific accusations. As a result, his society locks him up:

> He grappled with the ugliest truth that he could lay his hand on, and compelled his adversary to do the same. Strange spectacle in human life, where it is the instinctive effort of one and all to hide those sad

realities, and leave them undisturbed beneath a heap of superficial topics, which constitute the materials of intercourse between man and man! It was not to be tolerated that Roderick Elliston should break through the tacit compact, by which the world has done its best to secure repose, without relinquishing evil. (10:277–278).

Once confined, Roderick tries to drown his self-loathing with tobacco, then liquor, then drugs. They all nurture the snake.

Finally, Roderick is released and studies a useless intellectual analysis of snakes when his friend Herkimer asks if there is a cure. Roderick replies that he need only forget himself. At this announcement, Roderick's wife, Rosina, appears and urges him to forget himself "in the idea of another!" (10:283)—namely, herself. Roderick and Rosina reconcile, and the snake disappears into the fountain in Roderick's backyard.

When Herkimer questions the completeness of Roderick's cure, Rosina assures him "with a heavenly smile," "The serpent was but a dark fantasy, and what it typified was as shadowy as itself. The past, dismal as it seems, shall fling no gloom upon the future. To give it its due importance, we must think of it but as an anecdote in our Eternity!" (10:283). As in other tales, a forgiving woman urges a self-absorbed man to trust her and, thus, himself. As in "The Man of Adamant," this tale associates salvation with water, and with a woman who urges a man trapped in arrogance to have faith in himself and others, beginning with her. Nor does Rosina discount Roderick's embarrassing past; it happened, but he can outgrow it. Most critics see the tale as a warning against the dangers of egocentricity.

This solution separates Roderick from society; after all, his contemporaries ignore their snakes. The story's imagery supports this distinction since Roderick's house stands back from the main street and he enjoys his final cure in "a shadowy enclosure in the rear of the mansion, where a student, or a dreamer, or a man of stricken heart, might lie all day upon the grass, amid the solitude of murmuring boughs, and forget that a city had grown up around him" (10:280–281). Roderick inherited this house from ancestors who also had snakes. So Roderick's family and his society both encourage the self-absorption responsible for his malaise; to heal, he must retreat, relax, and feel. Since moving beyond egotism requires him to accept his frailty and his goodness without judging either, he must put aside conventional judgments as well as his own. As the tale ends, Rosina begins to show him how.

"Earth's Holocaust"

"Earth's Holocaust" elaborates on the limitations and interdependence of social codes and self-reliance. This story describes a group of reformers who burn cultural icons to rid themselves of unfair institutions. The narrator establishes his unreliability at the start by explaining his love of fires, and the hope "that the illumination of the bonfire might reveal some profundity of moral truth, heretofore hidden in mist or darkness," draws him to this event. Once he arrives, he certifies his passivity by habitually adopting the opinion of one man who "struck me immediately as having weighed for himself the true value of life and its circumstances, and therefore as feeling little personal interest in whatever judgment the world might form of them" (10:381–382).

The narrator's vacuity serves the tale because it makes him a reporter, not an interpreter. As a result, the story presents a multitude of confusing, contradictory views, reinforcing its theme: truth resists easy, clear judgment. When the narrator does reach a conclusion, he gives the reader ample reason to discount it.

Throughout the tale, symbols of institutions such as churches and governments get tossed into the bonfire. As the flames devour each set of tokens, someone with a vested interest in the canon they represent protests that this convention keeps people civil. Since the narrator's mentor remains unpersuaded by these arguments, so does the narrator, until books disappear into the flames.

The narrator is, after all, a writer. He even risks voicing an objection, but then stands aside to let others speak. When a critic proclaims, "Writers will henceforth be compelled to light their lamps at the sun or stars," the narrator replies, appropriately, "If they can reach so high . . . but that task requires a giant, who may afterwards distribute the light among inferior men. It is not every one that can steal the fire from Heaven, like Prometheus; but when once he had done the deed, a thousand hearths were kindled by it" (10:396). Institutions not only oppress the best of human history, they can preserve and encourage it.

The narrator's bravery does not last. When another author protests, the narrator's hero calls him a "book-worm," and the narrator finishes the argument: "Is not Nature better than a book?—is not the human heart deeper than any system of philosophy?" (10:398). Both conclusions make sense. The tale shows that one cannot make accurate, one-sided judgments of human institutions.

Meanwhile, the reformers continue to incinerate cultural artifacts, unimpeded by reflection. The irrationality of the conflagration becomes more overt as the tale continues; eventually, stymied in their search for more symbols to burn, the reformers toss leaves into the fire. Finally, a "dark-complexioned personage . . . [whose] eyes glowed with a redder light than that of the bonfire" announces evil is safe; the human heart remains: "Unless they hit upon some method of purifying that foul cavern, forth from it will re-issue all the shapes of wrong and misery" (10:403). The narrator realizes the wisdom of this statement and so do the critics. Most identify this judgment as the tale's theme.

But earlier, the observer calmed down the narrator as the Bible turned to ash by reminding him, "The world of tomorrow will again enrich itself with the gold and diamonds, which have been cast off by the world of to-day. Not a truth is destroyed—nor buried so deep among the ashes, but it will be raked up at last." When the Bible does not burn, the narrator accepts this conclusion: "I beheld, among the wallowing flames, a copy of the Holy Scriptures, the pages of which, instead of being blackened into tinder, only assumed a more dazzling whiteness, as the finger-marks of human imperfection were purified away" (10:402).

The narrator's indecisiveness leads him to embrace, not only contradiction, but truth. Both good and evil will survive as long as the human race; the institutions people create reflect and reinforce both. One cannot choose between conformity and individualism or between good and evil, because they intertwine. This judgment further validates Mary Goffe's wisdom, for if one cannot separate good from evil, it makes sense to accept strength and weakness in oneself and others. Hawthorne recommends trusting all sides of oneself, trusting all elements of others, and trusting, finally, that embracing complication will redeem one's life.

"The Ambitious Guest"

"The Ambitious Guest" elaborates on the wisdom and nature of the accepting stance. The title character, determined not to die unknown, "had travelled far and alone; his whole life, indeed, had been a solitary path; for, with the lofty caution of his nature, he had kept himself apart from those who might otherwise have been his companions." He seeks fame after death: "When posterity should gaze back into the gloom of what was now the present, they would trace the brightness of his footsteps, brightening as meaner glories faded, and confess, that a gifted one had passed from his cradle to his tomb, with none to recognize him." The young man has a truly "high and abstracted ambition," for it has no content other than posthumous recognition of his superiority. His look of "melancholy . . . almost despondency" (9:325–328) shows his aspirations have not made him happy. And why would they? They assert little except his separation from other people.

The family running the inn epitomizes a serenity opposite of the young man's questing stance. They live on the side of a mountain constantly threatening them with avalanche. Yet the story opens describing their peace: "The faces of the father and mother had a sober gladness; the children laughed; the eldest daughter was the image of Happiness at seventeen; and the aged grandmother, who sat knitting in the warmest place, was the image of Happiness grown old. They had found the 'herb, heart's ease,' in the bleakest spot of all New-England" (9:324). Their warmth and acquiescence bring them joy. The family easily absorbs the travelers stopping at their inn: "It was one of those primitive taverns, where the traveller pays only for food and lodging, but meets with a homely kindness, beyond all price." When the Ambitious Guest enters, "the whole family rose up . . . as if about to welcome some one who belonged to them" (9:325). As soon as he sees them, the anguish disappears from his face.

Encouraged by their kindness, he begins to share his dreams with them and they respond sympathetically. Although at first they have trouble understanding his goal, eventually they begin articulating their own. As they turn from the present and each other to future hopes and fears, the mood shifts from contentment to anxiety. Then the avalanche begins. The family flees to the shelter they think will protect them, but they all perish. The avalanche bypasses their house; if they had stayed home, they would have survived. One could link their deaths to their ambition, and a number of critics have. On the other hand, when someone passing by seems to call his name, the innkeeper does not go because he "was unwilling to show himself too solicitous of gain" (9:330). One of the children berates his family for missing this opportunity for a ride to the Flume and everyone laughs. But had the family left, perhaps they would have lived. So the tale can also be seen as affirming aspirations or even the intuitive wisdom of childhood.

These apparently conflicting readings meld into one: the inability of human beings to govern their fate renders pointless their obsession with achieving goals. Another cluster of commentators takes this view of the tale, among them Ray B. Browne: "The theme is not only the futility of personal ambition . . . ; rather it is the larger theme of man's weakness in the hands of indifferent fate and the impossibility of avoiding disaster."[6]

Most people, like the young man, try to shape their lives into something extraordinary. But, like the young man, they live to die. He shuts down feelings that could enrich his present to protect a future he won't enjoy. The family members have dreams, but they also enjoy whatever and whomever enter their lives. This responsiveness allows them to identify with the guest's despair. Their sympathy makes them sad, but also teaches them about themselves.

The tale's denouement shows that since people cannot control their lives, devoting oneself to the realization of a grand plan harms rather than enriches. The family, who had only feeble aspirations to greatness, achieves the fame the guest sought. Their renown grows from the human attachments he thought would hold him back: "All had left separate tokens, by which those, who had known the family, were made to shed a tear for each. Who has not heard their name? The story has been told far and wide, and will forever be a legend of these mountains" (11:333). As for the young man, some people think there was a guest, but others dispute this claim. He dies unknown.

So "The Ambitious Guest" shows that when people commit themselves to a goal instead of trusting their emotional responses to each moment and circumstance, they undermine the present and delay fulfillment of their desires. In all Hawthorne's tales, characters rarely shape lives matching their aims. Those who sacrifice their feelings to community standards wind up isolated. Those who ignore others to concentrate on individual achievement end up unhappy. Moreover, both conformists and individualists make their lives a battleground. In selecting one option, they do not eliminate the opposing impulses, but shove them underground. Suppressed feelings do not die, but make themselves felt, again and again. Those who accept all of themselves, including their limits, can listen to and embrace other flawed human beings. Openness not only brings peace, it enhances every moment of their lives.

Artists and Scientists

Maintaining a healthy balance between self-esteem and humility challenges everyone, but this task poses particular problems for those whose work assumes extraordinary insight. The scientist looks beyond the known, while the artist articulates a unique point of view; both expose new aspects of reality. Artists and scientists must cultivate their distinctive ways of seeing, but this puts them at risk for arrogance. And the same discernment making them good artists and scientists will destroy their craft if not balanced by awareness of their frailty.

"The Birth-mark"

Aylmer of "The Birth-mark" is an accomplished scientist, but he aspires to divinity. He hints that, if he put his mind to it, he could create a human being, invent water to prolong life, and make gold. His notebooks reveal that he has consistently brought noble ambitions to his scientific experiments and, just as consistently, failed: "The volume, rich with achievements that had won renown for its author, was yet as melancholy a record as ever mortal hand had penned. It was the sad confession, and continual exemplification, of the short-comings of the composite man—the spirit burdened with clay and working in matter—and of the despair that assails the higher nature, at finding itself so miserably thwarted by the earthly part" (10:49). Aylmer's confidence suggests he rarely reviews his journals.

Aylmer washes off the laboratory dirt, takes a break from science, and falls in love with Georgiana, a beautiful woman with a birthmark. People's reactions to this blemish reflect their points of view. Women jealous of Georgiana's beauty virulently criticize it, but men, "if the birth-mark did not heighten their admiration, contented themselves with wishing it away, that the world might possess one living specimen of ideal loveliness, without the semblance of a flaw" (10:38). The narrator sides with the men, saying that to claim the mark destroys Georgiana's beauty would be as if "one of those small blue stains, which sometimes occur in the purest statuary marble, would convert the Eve of Powers to a monster" (10:38).

But Aylmer assumes this irrational point of view. After their marriage, he becomes increasingly obsessed with the birthmark, seeing it as a symptom of frailty he must conquer: "The Crimson Hand expressed the ineludible gripe, in which mortality clutches the highest and purest of earthly mould, degrading them into kindred with the lowest, and even with the very brutes, like whom their visible frames return to dust" (10:39). This flaw symbolizes the impotence even Aylmer's scientific knowledge cannot circumvent.

By removing it, Aylmer secretly hopes to prove that nothing, not even death, lies beyond the correction of his science. Thus, the blemish becomes associated with fear; what Aylmer considers a "frightful object" (10:39) shows up on Georgiana's cheek only when she pales. Because making the mark vanish will establish Aylmer's omnipotence, he tells Georgiana: "You have led me deeper than ever into the heart of science. I feel myself fully competent to render this dear cheek as faultless as its fellow; and then, most beloved, what will be my triumph, when I shall have corrected what Nature left imperfect, in her fairest work!" (10:41).

Aylmer's assistant, Aminadab, executes all the physical tasks, freeing Aylmer to cultivate delusions of transcendence: "With his [Aminadab's] vast strength, his shaggy hair, his smoky aspect, and the indescribable earthiness that incrusted him, he seemed to represent man's physical nature; while Aylmer's slender figure, and pale, intellectual face, were no less apt a type of the spiritual element" (10:43).

The first time Aylmer shows his aversion to the birthmark, Georgiana angrily asks why he married her. But as their relationship continues, she absorbs his revulsion to it. So she learns to depise her own humanity, eventually becoming more vehement than Aylmer about removing the blemish: "Is this beyond your power, for the sake of your own peace, and to save your poor wife from madness?" (10:41). Georgiana may well stand at the edge of madness, for her relationship with Aylmer demands she mediate a formidable battle between self-esteem and self-hate.

While he tries to remove the mark, Aylmer puts Georgiana in an elegant, fantastic room that hides the crudity of his scientific experiments: "For aught Georgiana knew, it might be a pavilion among the clouds" (10:44). He also disguises his frustration when the blemish resists his cure. As the treatment drags on, he tries to distract Georgiana with a few scientific tricks. Even these trifles fail, but Aylmer "soon . . . forgot these mortifying failures" (10:46) and continues trying to perfect his wife. Georgiana eventually understands he may destroy her, but identifies so strongly with his loathing of imperfection, she would rather die than live with the birthmark.

She attributes this self-destructive attitude to the inspiring influence of Aylmer's high standards and urges him to continue his noble work, at any cost: "Life is but a sad possession to those who have attained precisely the degree of moral advancement at which I stand. Were I weaker and blinder, it might be happiness" (10:53). Because she identifies with Aylmer's arrogant and unrealistic expectations, Georgiana hates herself for being human.

Aylmer finally removes the spot, and Georgiana dies, reassuring Aylmer of his greatness: "My poor Aylmer! . . . You have aimed loftily!—

you have done nobly! Do not repent, that, with so high and pure a feeling, you have rejected the best that earth could offer" (10:55).

The narrator does not view Aylmer so positively, suggesting he would have done better to accept frailty: "Had Aylmer reached a profounder wisdom, he need not thus have flung away the happiness, which would have woven his mortal life of the self-same texture with the celestial." If Aylmer had achieved genuine idealism, he would have looked beyond material reality, including his wife's physical flaw, and attended to her spirit: "The momentary circumstance was too strong for him; he failed to look beyond the shadowy scope of Time, and, living once for all in Eternity, to find the perfect Future in the present" (10:56). Most of the tale's commentators identify this concluding generalization as the story's theme.

Aylmer must ignore all but the material to sustain the illusion of total control; since science shapes only the tangible world, he must persuade himself none other exists. His benighted perspective makes him a failure both as a scientist and as a human being; he kills his wife, first emotionally, then physically. But Georgiana's absorption of Aylmer's point of view shows the power of both science and arrogance; people so yearn to transcend human limits, they will destroy themselves rather than reconcile themselves to imperfection.

"Ethan Brand"

"Ethan Brand" presents another scientist whose pride leads him astray. Ethan Brand, a lime burner, gets the notion he can discover the Unpardonable Sin. Inspired by this goal, he cultivates his intellect: "The Idea that possessed his life had operated as a means of education; it had gone on cultivating his powers to the highest point of which they were susceptible; it had raised him from the level of an unlettered laborer, to stand on a star-lit eminence, whither the philosophers of the earth, laden with the lore of universities, might vainly strive to clamber after him." But while developing his mind, he buries his feelings: "So much for the intellect! But where was the heart? That, indeed, had withered—had contracted—had hardened—had perished! It ceased to partake of the universal throb" (11:99). Brand realizes he has lost his capacity for sympathy and proclaims this the unpardonable sin. Most critics agree that Brand's judgment of himself constitutes the tale's central theme.

Brand returns to the lime kiln where his search began and announces he has found the unpardonable sin in his own breast. But, his discovery pleases him: "Freely, were it to do again, would I incur the guilt. Unshrinkingly, I accept the retribution!" (11:90). Brand then proves he means it: he jumps into the flames associated with the devil and his reflections, incinerating himself.

As many critics have noted, the tale supports the common Christian notion that no unpardonable sin exists.[7] When a showman with a diorama invites Brand to look at the unpardonable sin, there is apparently nothing there. Almost simultaneously, a dog begins chasing his own tail, making Brand laugh in recognition of the analogy between the dog's pointless search and his own. In terms of Christian doctrine, Brand probably does die unpardoned, not because of behavior so horrific it rests beyond the reach of grace, but because he does not repent. From beginning to end, Brand harms himself.

The lack of brotherhood he claims deserves no mercy pervades Brand's community. Bartram, the present lime burner, greets Brand by threatening to throw marble at him. When Brand begins talking of his sin, Bartram feels uncomfortable sympathy: "The lime-burner's own sins rose up within him, and made his memory riotous with a throng of evil shapes that asserted their kindred with the Master Sin, whatever it might be, which it was within the scope of man's corrupted nature to conceive and cherish. They were all of one family; they went to and fro between his breast and Ethan Brand's, and carried dark greetings from one to the other" (11:88).

When Bartram finds Brand's skeleton, complete with intact heart, he smashes it, calculating its market value: "Was the fellow's heart made of marble? . . . At any rate, it is burnt into what looks like special good lime; and, taking all the bones together, my kiln is half a bushel the richer for him" (11:102). Earlier the narrator explained that although Bartram lacks Brand's intellectual development, he too has limits: "The man, who now watched the fire, was of a different order, and troubled himself with no thoughts save the very few that were requisite to his business" (11:85). Bartram uses people to make money as virulently as Brand manipulates others to gain knowledge. Bartram, too, can expect no mercy: he not only fails to repent, he does not admit his sin.

Smoke tinges all the townspeople. As many critics have noted, the townspeople not only share the Faustian imagery associated with Brand, they also lack brotherhood. They stare at and judge Brand. When he begins talking of his discoveries, they urge him to shut up and have a drink, their solution for life's dilemmas. No wonder when Brand sees them, "It made him doubt—and, strange to say, it was a painful doubt—

whether he had indeed found the Unpardonable Sin, and found it within himself." (11:93).

Why does this doubt pain Brand? Because he wants to succeed. If he can achieve preeminence in no other way, at least he can become an outstanding sinner. As Nina Baym explains: "It is certain, then, that Brand will do something eventually which will enable him to believe himself extraordinarily evil, unique among sinners. Having committed a crime which satisfies him, he devotes his energies alternately to advertising his great evil and to fighting off fears that he is self-deluded. He returns in a state of grim satisfaction to commit himself to the flames."[8] In Brand, Hawthorne creates a paradigm of self-destructive perfectionism; Brand ruins himself as surely as Aylmer kills Georgiana.

The townspeople's unkindnesses also hurt them, but rather than obsessing about their weaknesses, they drown them in drink and tobacco. This, too, isolates them, but they gather in pseudo-fellowship to pass the bottle. And, as flawed as they are, like Lawyer Giles, they struggle to live: "A maimed and miserable wretch he was; but one, nevertheless, whom the world could not trample on, and had no right to scorn, either in this or any previous stage of his misfortunes, since he had still kept up the courage and spirit of a man, asked nothing in charity, and, with his one hand—and that the left one—fought a stern battle against want and hostile circumstances" (11:91–92).

Occasionally, they even do good, like the alcoholic village doctor: "There was supposed to be in him such wonderful skill, such native gifts of healing, beyond any which medical science could impart, that society caught hold of him, and would not let him sink out of its reach" (11:92).

The kindness of Joey, Bartram's young son, implies human beings enter the world equipped with empathy. Richard Davison writes: "In Joey's sense of brotherhood perhaps is the hope of mankind: the ability to see beyond one's smoky self-identity and break through man's solipsistic wall of isolation. For Joey is the only rational human being in Hawthorne's story that seems aware of man's essential dignity."[9] When Joey hears Brand's laugh, it frightens him. When he meets Brand, he pities him. And when Brand dies, Joey recognizes that nature seems pleased. While Brand is associated with fire, and the townspeople with smoke, Joey is aligned with nature so pure it seems celestial: "Stepping from one to another of the clouds that rested on the hills, and thence to the loftier brotherhood that sailed in air, it seemed almost as if a mortal man might thus ascend into the heavenly regions. Earth was so mingled with sky that it was a day-dream to look at it" (11:101).

Brand once shared in the natural generosity animating Joey: "He [Brand] remembered how the night-dew had fallen upon him—how the dark forest had whispered to him—how the stars had gleamed upon him—a simple and loving man, watching his fire in the years gone by, and ever musing as it burned. He remembered with what tenderness, with what love and sympathy for mankind, and what pity for human guilt and wo, he had first begun to contemplate those ideas which afterwards became the inspiration of his life" (11:98). Brand knows he has split with nature even more profoundly than with other people: "'Oh, Mother Earth,' cried he, 'who art no more my Mother, and into whose bosom this frame shall never be resolved! Oh, mankind, whose brotherhood I have cast off, and trampled thy great heart beneath my feet!'" (11:100).

Their hope makes the lawyer and the doctor more admirable than Brand, and Joey the story's most sympathetic character. Brand's despair prevents repentance; instead, he embraces his isolation and the outstanding achievement it brings him. And Bartram clutches the valuable lime Brand leaves behind.

This tale shows that when human beings renounce their humanity for scientific control, they become so absorbed in proving their superiority, they destroy themselves. Like Brand and Bartram, they sacrifice their sensitivity to productivity. Those who evade knowledge may seem lazy and escapist, but at least they retain glimmerings of decency and hope.

This is a tragic tale. It suggests that human beings enter life with a deep fund of compassion, like Joey, but that as they age, they strive to control rather than love nature, others, and themselves. As their expertise grows, their humanity withers.

"Dr. Heidegger's Experiment"

"Dr. Heidegger's Experiment" places issues and situations found in "The Birth-mark" and "Ethan Brand" in an apparently lighthearted context. Dr. Heidegger is Aylmer grown old: he kills his fiancée with one of his prescriptions, uses science to play magician, and has a reputation for consorting with witches.

Heidegger shares Aylmer's confidence that he can reverse natural processes with the same result: bad science putting others at risk. Heidegger's subjects are all elderly people whose youthful errors ruined their lives. He gives them water from the Fountain of Youth, first urging them to pledge they will avoid repeating their mistakes. They laugh at the suggestion, drink the water, become young again, and replicate the stupidities that destroyed them. The politician wrecked by scandal mouths empty political phrases, including "some perilous stuff or other, in a sly and doubtful whisper, so cautiously that even his own conscience could scarcely catch the secret." The Colonel whose raucous behavior ruined his health, sings drinking songs and eyes the resuscitated Widow Wyncherly. The businessman who lost his fortune in speculation talks of "a project for supplying the East Indies with ice, by harnessing a team of whales to the polar icebergs" (9:234). And they all fight over the Widow, as they did years before. They forget where these actions will take them because, like most young people, they assume they will never suffer the indignity of old age: "The most singular effect of their gayety was an impulse to mock the infirmity and decrepitude of which they had so lately been the victims" (9:235–236).

All the while, Dr. Heidegger watches them. When the water wears off, he judges them: "Yes, friends, ye are old again, . . . and lo! the Water of Youth is all lavished on the ground. Well—I bemoan it not; for if the fountain gushed at my very doorstep, I would not stoop to bathe my lips in it—no, though its delirium were for years instead of moments. Such is the lesson ye have taught me!" (9:238). Most critics accept Heidegger's judgment as the tale's theme.

Dr. Heidegger could as easily have moralized about age's wisdom coming to everyone, for when elderly, even these foolish people regret their shallow youths. But that precept might console his friends. The nastiness of Heidegger's verdict seems consistent with experimenting on four vulnerable people. Heidegger even implies he chose people doomed to make fools of themselves. When they protest they would never repeat their errors, he says: "I rejoice that I have so well selected the subjects of my experiment" (9:232).

Heidegger's experiment hurts his subjects. When the Widow sees herself age, she "clasped her skinny hands before her face, and wished that the coffin-lid were over it, since it could be no longer beautiful" (9:238). Heidegger's victims spend the rest of their lives like unrepentant drug addicts, seeking the fountain of youth.

With this tale, Hawthorne extends his list of grievances against scientific vanity. As in "The Birth-mark," arrogance produces bad science, for people who think they can control physical reality overreach; they try to become magicians. But this story most passionately condemns the influence of scientific inquiry on character. While Aylmer also treated Georgiana like a thing and Brand confesses he did the same to his subjects, the objectifying aspect of the scientific attitude becomes clearest in "Dr. Heidegger's Experiment." Dr. Heidegger treats his so-called friends cruelly, and with objectivity. To learn from them, he uses them. Moreover, his science reinforces the endemic assumption that only externals matter. The Widow and her three suitors destroy their lives by overemphasizing looks, prestige, pleasure, and money. Science, with its promise of material transformation, feeds these delusions. Naturally, Heidegger's friends spend the rest of their lives seeking eternal youth.

In this tale, the physical damage wrought by bad science seems slight compared to the harm done by the scientific perspective. The scientist identifies objectivity with truth; when he treats other human beings from this stance, he turns them into things. Thus, reverence for science becomes a dehumanizing influence.

In general, Hawthorne's tales about scientists argue that intellectual facility producing good science can destroy if acknowledgement of frailty does not balance pride. Hawthorne's failure to describe a kind scientist suggests pessimism about the possibility of achieving superior mental development without losing one's compassion. The easy capitulation of others to the scientist's materialism does not bode well for the modern age. Indeed, Hawthorne's tales anticipate warnings about the limits of science raised repeatedly in the twentieth century by existentialists, psychologists, theologians, sociologists, and even scientists themselves.

Although "Dr. Heidegger's Experiment" describes a tragic series of events strikingly similar to those in "The Birth-mark" and "Ethan Brand," these tales have a somber tone, while "Dr. Heidigger's Experiment" drips with sarcasm. The narrator shares Heidegger's amusement at the humiliation of his friends; he pronounces Heidegger's subjects "Old creatures . . . whose greatest misfortune it was, that they were not long ago in their graves" (9: 227). He extends his contempt to Dr. Heidegger and all other elderly people: "Dr. Heidegger and all his four guests were sometimes thought to be a little beside themselves; as is not unfrequently the case with old people, when worried either by present troubles or woful recollections" (9:228). Then he repeats embarrassing rumors about Heidegger, admitting "some of these fables, to my shame be it spoken, might possibly be traced back to mine own veracious self" (9:229–230).

The narrator observes along with Heidegger, recording the disappointment of his subjects with little sympathy. So the tale's narrator, like

Heidegger, watches, judges, and uses people with no compassion.[10] In other tales, Hawthorne elaborates on the ways artists' vanity can lead them into the same destructive patterns as scientists.

"The Artist of the Beautiful"

Owen Warland of "The Artist of the Beautiful" hates his age's pragmatism as virulently as his society despises creativity. An artist forced to train as a watchmaker, Owen repeatedly attempts to complete a private creative project. Hostile comments from the blacksmith, Robert Danforth, and Peter Hovenden, the person who taught Owen watch repair, continually interfere with Owen's work. Annie Hovenden, the secret love of Owen's life, responds more kindly, but when he allows her to touch his work, she destroys it. The entire plot of "The Artist of the Beautiful" consists of Owen's struggle to sustain his artistic integrity in a society populated by materialists.

Owen tries repeatedly to renounce his work. He conforms for a time, becoming a meticulous watchmaker. Then he comes into some money, tries a dissolute life, and satisfies his fantasies with alcoholic dreams. And later, he becomes childlike, living in his imagination. But he always goes back to work. He finally completes and unveils his achievement: a mechanical butterfly. He presents his invention to Anne Hovenden, and they both watch her child destroy it. The narrator explains that Owen remains unperturbed because "when the artist rose high enough to achieve the Beautiful, the symbol by which he made it perceptible to mortal senses became of little value in his eyes, while his spirit possessed itself in the enjoyment of the Reality" (10:475). Most critics see this as Owen's moment of artistic triumph over society's materialism. As Thelma Shinn puts it: "Owen has achieved the pure spiritual vision of the ideal and has recreated it as much as possible in earthly materials."[11]

Despite Owen's long and noble struggle, the triviality of his product makes it hard to see him as heroic. A sizable number of critics agree, among them John Stubbs: "The narrowness of what Owen has accomplished, the escapist nature of his absorption, and the isolation inherent in his role are all factors which Hawthorne uses to qualify his defense of Owen."[12]

The narrator's ambiguity about Owen's achievement makes it impossible to wholeheartedly endorse it.[13] The narrator's orations on the value of art and the shallowness of ordinary folk establishes his sympathy for the artist. One cannot doubt the idealism of a narrator who talks like this:

"Ideas which grow up within the imagination, and appear so lovely to it, and of a value beyond whatever men call valuable, are exposed to be shattered and annihilated by contact with the Practical. It is requisite for the ideal artist to possess a force of character that seems hardly compatible with its delicacy; he must keep faith in himself, while the incredulous world assails him with its utter disbelief" (10:454). This same narrator says the townspeople may be right: Owen may have lost his mind. When Owen finally produces the butterfly, the narrator seems less than ecstatic: "It was his fortune, good or ill, to achieve the purpose of his life" (10:468). When Annie clearly prefers her child to Owen's butterfly, the narrator thinks she shows good judgment. At best, the tale is ambiguous about Owen's accomplishment.

The story's frame makes it even more difficult to admire Owen. The tale opens with Peter Hovenden's comment that all Owen could hope to create was a "Dutch toy": "He would turn the sun out of its orbit, and derange the whole course of time, if . . . his ingenuity could grasp anything bigger than a child's toy!" (10:448). And, finally, Owen's efforts produce a child's toy. When he sees it, Peter Hovenden sneers, and Hovenden's grandchild destroys it wearing the same cynical smile.

Owen tries to make machinery look natural; like Aylmer, Owen attempts to reshape what reminds him of his limits. Like Aylmer, he deludes himself into believing love motivates him, but Annie's lack of sympathy establishes this so-called love as escapist fantasy: "In the aspect which she wore to his inward vision, [Annie] was as much a creation of his own, as the mysterious piece of mechanism" (10:464). In fact, Owen's hatred of the machine inspires him. Owen's art, like Aylmer's science, is a hopeless attempt to evade reality. Owen's art is a toy.

His creation complements his personality, for he lacks depth. When in crisis, he gets drunk, conforms, or babbles. Throughout the story, he resembles a petulant child irritated by reality's demands. During his happiest period, he does not work, but wanders the countryside, letting images pass in and out of his brain: "Sweet, doubtless, were these days, and congenial to the artist's soul. They were full of bright conceptions, which gleamed through his intellectual world, as the butterflies gleamed through the outward atmosphere, and were real to him for the instant, without the toil, and perplexity, and many disappointments, of attempting to make them visible to the sensual eye" (10:458). When Owen conquers material reality by making a machine resemble a butterfly, he remains happy after its destruction, because he retains his fantasies about it. Owen loves illusion, not art.

In this tale, Hawthorne shows that hostility to practical concerns does not make one an artist. To confuse escapist fantasies with art reduces it to a plaything. "The Artist of the Beautiful" not only talks about vacuous art, it gives the reader a sense of it though its chatty narrator. His long, abstract discussions of art and society put a veil between the reader and the characters. This tale does not engage its readers' feelings or senses, allowing them to both experience and observe art as a futile mind game.

"Wakefield"

The narrator of "Wakefield," like Owen Warland, has profound character flaws that limit his creation. He does not even pretend to ground his imaginings in reality. He fabricates a story from a newspaper article about a man the narrator calls Wakefield, who left his wife, moved into a nearby apartment, and let his wife assume he had disappeared. Twenty years later, he went home. The narrator knows if he muses about this episode, he will produce an illuminating story: "There will be a pervading spirit and a moral, even should we fail to find them, done up neatly, and condensed into the final sentence. Thought has always its efficacy, and every striking incident its moral" (9:131). His tale proves as substantial as Owen's butterfly.

The narrator begins by considering Wakefield's character and judges it weak. Lacking strong emotions or thoughts, Wakefield appears ordinary. Only his wife notices something unusual; the narrator identifies these outstanding characteristics as a "quiet selfishness," "a peculiar sort of vanity," "a disposition to craft" (9:132). After Wakefield leaves his wife with a murky account of when to expect him, she thinks he reopens the door and smirks at her. This incident prevents her from considering herself a widow during the next twenty years. Thus, Mrs. Wakefield establishes her reliability at the start of the story.

Wakefield seems a basic sadist. Emotionally empty, he has little sense of direction, but gets mild pleasure from hurting others. So he enjoys watching his house and monitoring his wife's reactions to his absence. Too numb to feel much, he "is excited to something like energy of feeling" (9:136) when seeing a doctor come from the house makes him wonder if his wife will die.

On some level, Wakefield recognizes his cruelty, so he spends his twenty years in paranoid terror. Eventually, he evolves into a lean, nervous person who walks down the street sideways: "He is meagre; his low and narrow forehead is deeply wrinkled; his eyes, small and lustreless, sometimes wander apprehensively about him, but oftener seem to look inward. He bends his head, and moves with an indescribable obliquity of gait, as if unwilling to display his full front to the world." Meanwhile, his wife grows "portly," "placid," and "well conditioned" (9:137). Administering cruelty does not assuage Wakefield's emptiness, nor does receiving it undermine his wife's calm. Eventually, Wakefield feels cold while passing his house, sees a comfortable fire and his wife's shadow through a window, and goes home.

The tale has a clear moral: changes in behavior alter little. Unhappy with the tedium of his life, Wakefield breaks from it. But he does not escape his emotional vacuity. Hope of vicariously appropriating Mrs. Wakefield's warmth may have drawn him to her; but as this project inevitably failed, he would feel only jealousy. Perhaps anticipating that her discomfort will resuscitate him, he leaves, and the possibility of her death gives him a slight thrill. Finally, however, the fates of Mr. and Mrs. Wakefield reflect their emotional attitudes; the event consuming twenty years of their lives influences little.

The narrator draws a different moral. He announces that the tale proves "amid the seeming confusion of our mysterious world, individuals are so nicely adjusted to a system, and systems to one another, and to a whole, that, by stepping aside for a moment, a man exposes himself to a fearful risk of losing his place forever. Like Wakefield, he may become, as it were, the Outcast of the Universe" (9:140). The majority of critics accept this judgment as the story's theme.

More recent commentators recognize that this moral makes no sense, but the narrator does fulfill his promise to supply a lesson "even should we fail to find [one]" (9:131). As Robert Chibka notes: "The first paragraph, so devoid of moral or psychological cause and effect, instills a desire for the golden world where everything *means*; the remainder of the tale exemplifies, even as it professes to condemn, the self-enclosed and potentially self-defeating mentality that proceeds from and strives to fulfill that desire."[14]

The evidence proving Wakefield an Outcast of the Universe is, despite the emphatic capital letters, not clear. At the beginning of the story, the narrator says Wakefield "entered the door one evening, quietly, as from a day's absence, and became a loving spouse till death" (9:130). As the tale closes, the narrator describes Wakefield's return as "this happy event" (9:140). The narrator also concludes that Wakefield can never return home because he has so violently sundered his relationship with Mrs. Wakefield. But there was little to break. Before he leaves, "his matrimonial affections, never violent, were sobered into a calm, habitual sentiment" (9:131). Indeed, perhaps twenty years of walking sideways in a red wig has enhanced his affection for Mrs. Wakefield. Wakefield's behavior doesn't isolate him, his emotional emptiness does.

The narrator does not want to face this moral because he needs to distinguish himself from Wakefield. As the story opens, he asserts Wakefield's uniqueness and claims that Wakefield's originality, along with his own innate kindness, draw him to this episode: "The incident, though of the purest originality, unexampled, and probably never to be repeated, is one, I think, which appeals to the general sympathies of mankind." Little ties Wakefield's story to sympathy except, perhaps, the narrator's next sentence: "We know, each for himself, that none of us would perpetrate such a folly, yet feel as if some other might" (9:130–131). The narrator not only manages to contradict his assertion of the event's uniqueness, he reveals why he needs to believe that "general sympathies" attract him to Wakefield's story. Selfishness distinguishes Wakefield; the narrator must establish he does not share it.

The tale illuminates the narrator's resemblance to Wakefield. Like Wakefield, he sets out without any sense of direction, but certain that something fine will come from his expedition. Instead, the narrative, like Wakefield's journey, lacks coherence. With no inner dynamic to pull the plot forward, the narrator intercedes now and then to give it a push: "Let us now imagine Wakefield bidding adieu to his wife" (9:132); "But, our business is with the husband. We must hurry after him, along the street, ere he lose his individuality, and melt into the great mass of London life" (9:133); "Now for a scene!" (9:137). The narrator has no more control of his story than Wakefield has of his life and for the same reason: neither has enough substance to form a consistent plan.

The narrator sometimes claims moral significance for his narrative, but he also calls it a "long whim-wham," and the evil Wakefield a "crafty nincompoop" (9:135). Both Wakefield and the narrator lack an emotional center. And both attempt to fill this void by manipulating other people, but they cannot even formulate a purpose. So they just keep toying with others in the hope something will eventually come to them. It never does. Wakefield returns home having learned nothing and smirks at his wife because the same arrogance that freezes him renders him incapable of admitting failure. Simultaneously, the narrator ends his tale with no notion why he told it or what it means.

The narrator's lack of empathy not only produces incoherence, it makes his characters stick figures. The events and personages of this tale recede in the background as the reader watches the narrator shift judgments and language as he struggles to make up his mind. But until he, like Wakefield, admits his humanity, feels his emptiness, and admits his stupidity, he can write nothing with a genuine point or lively characters. "Wakefield" is the tale emotional aridity wrote. Through it, Hawthorne links artists who manipulate their characters and cruelty. That they work in the imagination does not protect them from blame. Nor does it redeem their lives or their work. Only rich characters produce rich art.

"The Prophetic Pictures"

The artist in "The Prophetic Pictures" shares essential characteristics with the narrator of "Wakefield." He is cold, arrogant, manipulative, and cultivates drama to give himself the illusion of vitality. His dress makes him look like he stepped from one of his portraits. He refuses to paint anyone with a "sleek and comfortable visage" (9:168). Instead, he wanders the countryside capturing "the glow of perilous moments; flashes of wild feeling; struggles of fierce power—love, hate, grief, frenzy" (9:178).

His colonial portraits all have something dramatic and negative about them. He paints Governor Burnett "inditing a most sharp response," and hangs the portrait next to the man who opposes him, Mr. Cooke. A picture of the lady of Sir William Phipps, "not unsuspected of witchcraft" (9:170), joins them. A two-hundred-year-old painting of a placid Madonna creates a sharp contrast to his work.

Nor can he capture nature's beauty: "He had been far enough to the north to see the silver cascade of the Crystal Hills . . . but he did not profane that scene by the mockery of his art" (9:177). Despite his extensive training, sublimity remains beyond his grasp. The opening paragraph announces his various expertises: he knows Hebrew and anatomy, and can "speak like a native of each clime and country on the globe, except our own forests" (9:166). Unfortunately, in Hawthorne's scheme, the ability to converse with nature is crucial to fine art.

All his other knowledge, as well as his ability to paint portraits resembling their subjects, invite the painter to cultivate a lethal vanity. When the painter decides he can predict the future and, thus, control time, the narrator declares him insane: "It is not good for man to cherish a solitary ambition. Unless there be those around him, by whose example he may regulate himself, his thoughts, desires, and hopes will become extravagant, and he the semblance, perhaps the reality, of a madman. Reading other bosoms, with an acuteness almost preternatural, the painter failed to see the disorder of his own" (9:180). The painter has a madness not unlike Aylmer's, and with similar consequences.

He paints portraits of an engaged couple, Walter and Elinor. At first glance, the paintings seem good resemblances, but those who look deeply see an ominous dimension. Elinor has nameless fears about Walter that her picture reveals. Walter's likeness has a lively quality compatible with his assaulting Elinor. The paintings finally bother Elinor and Walter so much they cover them. But the artist, anxious to know if his prediction has realized itself, goes to their home and reveals his priorities by asking the servant if the portraits are home.

The painter discovers the young couple standing before their uncovered pictures. Then Walter declares "Our fate is upon us! . . . Die!" and attacks Elinor with a knife. The painter stops Walter, "with the same sense of power to regulate their destiny, as to alter a scene upon the canvass. He stood like a magician, controlling the phantoms which he had evoked." The artist reminds Elinor of his warning, and she answers that she loved Walter. Then the narrator draws a moral: "Could the result of one, or all our deeds, be shadowed forth and set before us—some would call it Fate, and hurry onward—others be swept along by their passionate desires—and none be turned aside by the PROPHETIC PICTURES" (9:181–182). A number of critics see this pronouncement as the tale's theme.

A more significant motif seems the artist's tendency to forget her or his limits. And, indeed, a number of commentators see this as a tale about artistic arrogance. The association between magic and art plays a heavy role in the tragedy. Both those who condemn and those who revere the painter believe he has supernatural abilities:

> Some deemed it an offence against the Mosaic law, and even a presumptuous mockery of the Creator, to bring into existence such lively images of his creatures. Others, frightened at the art which could raise phantoms at will, and keep the form of the dead among the living, were inclined to consider the painter as a magician, or perhaps the famous Black Man of old witch-times, plotting mischief in a new guise. These foolish fancies were more than half believed, among the mob. Even in superior circles, his character was invested with a vague awe. (9:169)

Faith in his miraculous ability almost causes murder. In fact, the artist is human, although no one resists acknowledging it more than he.

In this tale, art expresses and reflects limited points of view. The emotionally sterile artist gives himself the illusion of vitality by focusing on human danger and conflict. His perspective shapes and restricts his work. The viewers' prejudices also enter in and create the painting. For instance, when Walter and Elinor look at the same portrait of Rev. Dr. Colman, Elinor sees his kindliness and Walter expects Rev. Dr. Colman to reprimand him, "But so does the original. I shall never feel quite comfortable under his eye, till we stand before him to be married!" (9:171). As Richard Robey notes, "The nature of things is exposed by a series of encounters with the portraits; they take life not from their essential nature, but from the interaction of a series of perspectives."[15] In this tale, beauty, doubt, terror, and murder all exist in the mind of the beholder.

Elinor feared Walter long before the painter recorded it. Had she faced her emotions, she could have resolved them. When the painter records her apprehension, she declares she will ignore it: "We will not have the pictures altered. . . . If mine is sad, I shall but look the gayer for the contrast'" (9:176). So the painter's inability to love gives him an arrogance that, along with superstition, convinces him of his preternatural ability. Elinor's unwillingness to face her fears allows them to overwhelm her. Although art cannot predict the future, it does present perspectives people can acknowledge and learn from. But regarding artists as prophets makes their creations potentially dangerous as well as potentially educative.

"Chippings with a Chisel"

The narrator of "Chippings with a Chisel," like the artist in "The Prophetic Pictures," thinks he has extraordinary insight, but, unlike the painter, the narrator has his views challenged, and he may even learn from this dialogue. The story consists of interactions between the narrator and a tombstone carver named Wigglesworth who spend a summer together on Martha's Vineyard. While the narrator just "summers" there, the carver makes tombstones for residents. This difference characterizes the two.

While the narrator stands back, watches, and judges events, the tombstone carver helps people resolve delicate and significant issues. The narrator considers himself superior to the earthy carver: "He was quite like a child in all matters save what had some reference to his own business; he seemed, unless my fancy mislead me, to view mankind in no other relation than as people in want of tomb-stones; and his literary

attainments evidently comprehended very little, either of prose or poetry, which had not, at one time or other, been inscribed on slate or
marble." But the narrator condescends to admit that the carver "had not
failed, within a narrow scope, to gather a few sprigs of earthly, and more
than earthly, wisdom—the harvest of many a grave" (9:409).

These introductory remarks warn the reader to suspect the narrator,
for he confesses that his fancy may mislead him. As the tale progresses, it
becomes harder to believe the narrator reports anything except his
ruminations. Moreover, the tombstone carver's concern for human mortality hardly seems trivial. And why would he need a literary background? Because narrators of short stories do? The narrator's opening
judgment betrays an egotism the rest of the tale confirms. Through the
dialogue between the carver and the narrator, this story offers a debate
between practical and spiritual art, suggesting wise people will side with
the carver. Wiggleworth's concern with human needs reveals a sensitivity that imbues his work, while the narrator's longing to establish his
superiority infects him and his tale.

The narrator wants to prove the carver his intellectual inferior. He has
the advantage in this contest, for he not only tells the story, he does not
risk embarrassing himself with action; he merely stands around making
pronouncements. Even with this edge, he loses.

The first tombstone purchase the narrator recalls involves a woman
whose lover died during her youth. She subsequently married and
enjoyed what seems a happy life. The narrator muses at length on the
death of her lover, concluding it deepened her values. As the following
excerpt demonstrates, he takes a long time to state this idea: "Amid the
throng of enjoyments, and the pressure of worldly care, and all the warm
materialism of this life, she had communed with a vision, and had been
the better for such intercourse. Faithful to the husband of her maturity,
and loving him with a far more real affection than she ever could have felt
for this dream of her girlhood, there had still been an imaginative faith to
the ocean-buried, so that an ordinary character had thus been elevated
and refined. Her sighs had been the breath of Heaven to her soul"
(9:410–411). And so on.

Still, she wants a tombstone commemorating what she considers "a
life-long sorrow" (9:410), with ocean plants and sea shells on it. Wigglesworth cannot carve anything that complex, so he persuades her to settle
for a rose with a broken stem. After she leaves, the narrator criticizes
the choice, and the carver defends it in a concise, concrete statement of
the same ideas the narrator developed at length: "That broken rose has

shed its sweet smell through forty years of the good woman's life" (9:411). The narrator ignores the carver's insightful comment. Instead, he moves on, telling of a man who orders three tombstones for his three deceased wives. His fourth wife accompanies him. Apparently anxious to condemn this man, the narrator watches to see if he favors any of his wives. When the man orders three identical tombstones, the narrator abandons this approach and judges the man for not respecting the individuality of his wives, proclaiming the questionable fairness of his judgment irrelevant: "There was even—if I wrong him, it is no great matter—a glance side-long at his living spouse, as if he were inclined to drive a thriftier bargain by bespeaking four grave-stones in a lot." The narrator prefers a whaling captain whose memory of his deceased wife "retained the bridal dew-drops" (9:411–412) because the captain spent little of their twenty-year marriage at home. Clearly, the narrator prefers fantasies to realities.

This bias for abstraction leads him into theoretical meanderings. He begins, for instance, reflecting on the phenomenon that husbands more often order tombstones for their deceased wives than widows for their spouses. At first, he suggests women remain so close to their husbands they can't bear the reminder. Then he hypothesizes a memorial may impede remarriage. Then he tells the story of a woman whose husband reappears while she oversees the chiseling of his stone. The narrator asks the carver how the woman reacted, and Wigglesworth says he felt sorry for her: "It was one of my best pieces of marble—and to be thrown away on a living man!" (9:413). In other words, the woman got more joy from memorializing her marriage than from living it. The narrator, too, gets pleasure from cultivating the illusion of reflection by tossing around abstractions about other people's lives. He would use his energy more profitably contemplating his own life.

When a woman and her daughter appear to select a tombstone for the girl's deceased twin sister, the narrator bounces between saying the sister knows intellectually, but not emotionally, her twin is dead, and concluding the sisters remain united. In the meantime, the carver tries to help the family select a stone. When they all decide on a clichéd verse, the narrator helpfully explains its appropriateness to the reader: "But, when we ridicule the triteness of monumental verses, we forget that Sorrow reads far deeper in them than we can, and finds a profound and individual purport in what seems so vague and inexpressive, unless interpreted by her. She makes the epitaph anew, though the self-same words may have served for a thousand graves" (9:414). Subsequently, we learn the narrator appropriated this insight from the carver.

After the mother and daughter leave, the narrator objects to the verse and the carver explains with characteristic concision, "These little old scraps of poetry . . . seem to stretch to suit a great grief, and shrink to fit a small one" (9:414). Intellectual abstractions matter less than the feelings responding to and interpreting them. Realizing this makes the carver willing to put an atheistic proclamation on a monument; he knows "when the grave speaks such falsehoods, the soul of man will know the truth by its own horror" (9:416).

The narrator's lack of feeling facilitates his vague ruminations. If his pretentious judgments reflect any emotion, it is anger. When a man comes to buy a tombstone for his lifelong enemy, the narrator hypothesizes that these two men in fact loved each other. The carver says: "I doubt whether their dust will mingle" (9:415), acknowledging that even though this hatred may come from twisted love, it will probably never resolve into kindness. For that to happen, the men must admit their mistakes. Similarly, even though the narrator's desperate attempts to defeat the carver probably grow from sadness at his distance from others, he probably will never own this sorrow. The carver's incredible patience with the narrator's assaults may stem from his recognition of the narrator's loneliness.

When the narrator attacks the bow and arrow the carver puts on an Indian's tombstone, saying it makes the tomb look like Cupid's, he admits he takes "a perverse view." Instead of getting defensive, the carver responds: "How can Cupid die when there are such pretty maidens in the Vineyard?" The narrator accepts the wisdom of this comment, and "for the rest of the day I thought of other matters than tomb-stones" (9:416). The carver seems to know the narrator criticizes because he can resolve his separateness only in fantasy.

At the end of the story, the narrator tells of a man too miserly and a girl too spiritual to have strong attachments, so they select their own monuments. Then the carver asks the narrator what kind of tombstone he wants, all but directly acknowledging the narrator's isolation. The same narrator who tells a story making consistent connections between gravestones and memories of loved ones decides he has no interest in monuments because they interfere with spirituality: "Every grave-stone that you ever made is the visible symbol of a mistaken system. Our thoughts should soar upward with the butterfly—not linger with the exuviae that confined him. . . . And to gain the truer conception of DEATH, I would fain forget the GRAVE!"

Owning the implications of selecting his own stone would force the narrator to reflect on his emptiness. He decides to evade the issue instead, so he forgets that graves reflect enduring bonds between people. The carver, who has responded generously to one criticism after another, loses patience with the narrator's obtuseness, actually challenging him: "Would you forget your dead friends, the moment they are under the sod!" (9:418).

As the tale closes, the narrator admits only confusion. He does confess learning from the carver, "And yet, with my gain of wisdom, I had likewise gained perplexity; for there was a strange doubt in my mind, whether the dark shadowing of this life, the sorrows and regrets, have not as much real comfort in them—leaving religious influences out of the question—as what we term life's joys" (9:418). The few critics who comment on the tale identify this statement as its moral. Although the carver has spent his life immersed in sorrow, it has made him joyful because he has met important needs with generosity and grace. The narrator has stood on life's sidelines, philosophizing and judging, but never risking connection. This stance leaves him with a loneliness he can paper over with intellectual assertions of superiority, but can cure only with emotional honesty.

Because the narrator lacks integrity, he not only has a lonely life, he produces bad art. His tale moves from one self-justifying rumination to the next, leaving the reader too removed from the events to care about them. The reader quickly learns that the narrator's attempt to avoid the knowledge that could redeem his life is the real story. Like "The Artist of the Beautiful," "Chippings with a Chisel" establishes that one cannot escape reality and create significant art. But the carver's wisdom shows practical awareness can help the artist face and address the deepest human longings and fears.

And the carver is named Wigglesworth. The narrator identifies him as a descendant of the Puritan author of "The Day of Doom." Thus, in affirming the carver's point of view, the tale suggests the Puritan obsession with sin, guilt, and mortality has value. So the story argues for not only acknowledging connections with others, but also honoring ties to the past. Owen Warland, the painter in "The Prophetic Pictures," and the narrators of "Chippings with a Chisel" and "Wakefield" expect to transcend death and society by retreating into self-indulgent fantasies. These tales show self-reliant artists, like arrogant scientists, may successfully delude themselves, but it will cost them their lives and their craft.

The narrator may represent a destructive historical shift. While tombstones built during colonial times have reminders of death on them, as the years have passed, gravestones look less morbid. This change may reflect a growing sense of human competence and control. If people come to assume, like the narrator of "Chippings with a Chisel," that they can conquer death, they may also share his pride, his detachment, and his unhappiness.

"Drowne's Wooden Image"

"Drowne's Wooden Image" explains why these emotionally sterile men produce bad art, for it identifies the genuine artist's strength as emotional. Drowne carves the best ship figureheads in the greater Boston area, but they all look alike. A craftsman rather than an artist, his mechanical approach reveals itself in his sculptures:

> It must be confessed, that a family likeness pervaded these respectable progeny of Drowne's skill—that the benign countenance of the king resembled those of his subjects, and that Miss Peggy Hobart, the merchant's daughter, bore a remarkable similitude to Britannia, Victory, and other ladies of the allegoric sisterhood; and, finally, that they all had a kind of wooden aspect, which proved an intimate relationship with the unshaped blocks of timber in the carver's workshop. But, at least, there was no inconsiderable skill of hand, nor a deficiency of any attribute to render them really works of art, except that deep quality, be it of soul or intellect, which bestows life upon the lifeless, and warmth upon the cold, and which, had it been present, would have made Drowne's wooden image instinct with spirit. (10:308–309)

Then Drowne carves a beautiful female figurehead everyone, even the painter Copley, recognizes as a work of art. The shift in Drowne's character when he shapes this lovely image helps define Hawthorne's view of the successful artist.

Drowne approaches this project humbly. When Copley compliments Drowne on his frozen statues, Drowne rejects the praise, pronouncing his earlier work deficient. This startles Copley, who now discovers an intelligence in Drowne's perspective, "though, hitherto, it had not given him greatly the advantage over his own family of wooden images"

(10:311). Copley reevaluates Drowne's work, suspecting he may have missed carvings of genuine beauty. When he reviews Drowne's completed carvings, he discovers nothing new, but the sculpture Drowne now fashions has a vitality his earlier productions lack. Copley asks where this image came from, and Drowne replies: "No man's work. . . . The figure lies within that block of oak, and it is my business to find it" (10:311). Drowne's reaction isolates another characteristic of the genuine artist, a submission to the materials and processes of art. Of course, Drowne uses his craftsmanship to mold the wood, but he accommodates to the oak's shapes and signals rather than imposing his preconceptions and goals on it.

As it becomes clearer Drowne produces a masterpiece, Copley urges him not to give it to the sea captain who commissioned it, but to sell it, unpainted, to a museum, for it has grown into a valuable piece of sculpture deserving kinder treatment than it would receive on a ship's prow. Drowne replies:

> "I know nothing of marble statuary, and nothing of a sculptor's rules of art. But of this wooden image—this work of my hands—this creature of my heart—" and here his voice faltered and choked, in a very singular manner—"of this—of her—I may say that I know something. A well-spring of inward wisdom gushed within me, as I wrought upon the oak with my whole strength, and soul, and faith! Let others do what they may with marble, and adopt what rules they choose. If I can produce my desired effect by painted wood, those rules are not for me, and I have a right to disregard them." (10:313)

Copley recognizes the appropriateness of Drowne's reaction and regrets his suggestion. Here, Hawthorne presents another characteristic of artists: they follow their intuitive sense of rightness rather than rules of the craft. Also, Drowne does not care how much money the figurehead earns him; the artist's delight in the process drives Drowne, not the craftman's desire to produce something meeting external standards and needs.

Drowne creates out of a love so intense Copley can see it: "He looked earnestly at Drowne, and again saw that expression of human love which, in a spiritual sense, as the artist could not help imagining, was the secret of the life that had been breathed into this block of wood" (10:314). The story's ending confirms this judgment, for a woman identical to the finished image appears, linking attachment to this human being and

Drowne's ability to transcend the mechanical practice of his craft. After Drowne completes this statue and the woman leaves town, he returns to making wooden images.

The narrator proclaims the story's probable moral:

> In every human spirit there is imagination, sensibility, creative power, genius, which, according to circumstances, may either be developed in this world, or shrouded in a mask of dulness until another state of being. To our friend Drowne, there came a brief season of excitement, kindled by love. It rendered him a genius for that one occasion, but, quenched in disappointment, left him again the mechanical carver in wood, without the power even of appreciating the work that his own hands had wrought.

The narrator hypothesizes that people are most themselves when they create passionately: "Yet who can doubt, that the very highest state to which a human spirit can attain, in its loftiest aspirations, is its truest and most natural state, and that Drowne was more consistent with himself when he wrought the admirable figure of the mysterious lady, than when he perpetrated a whole progeny of blockheads?" (10:319–320). Most critical interpretations of the tale develop one aspect or another of this judgment.

Drowne's love may have vicarious roots. At the beginning of the story, the ship captain who commissions the image selects the piece of wood Drowne carves. Drowne invites the captain to choose the form he wants imposed on the oak from the completed figureheads sitting around his workshop. Instead, the captain urges Drowne to make something new. Moreover, the woman who inspires the image lives at the captain's house. The tale offers no evidence Drowne ever sees her. Drowne's contact with the captain's desires and insights pushes him to create a work of art. Drowne has genius in him, but he needs external prompting to realize his gift. Once he fulfills the captain's orders, Drowne's creativity disappears.

On one hand, the tale shows how easily people ascend to creativity and how thoroughly they enjoy it. Drowne works in a dream. Everyone recognizes the magic of his work, even though his Puritan contemporaries suspect its extraordinary qualities: " 'One thing is certain,' muttered a Puritan of the old stamp. 'Drowne has sold himself to the devil' " (10:317). But Drowne realizes his artistic potential for only a moment. It requires the woman, the captain, the oak, and, most of all, Drowne's passion, to emerge. Works of art grow from emotion and they share its fragility. Community pressure mitigates against the vulnerability at the core of great art. Even Copley unconsciously swallows conventional standards. He proclaims rules to Drowne and advises him to get as much money as possible out of the statue, though he later realizes these ways of proceeding violate artistic integrity. Because societies feel comfortable with people who operate mechanically, and most want to fit, they sacrifice their individualism. Copley seeks out Drowne because, as an artist, he has so few people to talk with. And Drowne's community loves him the most fervently after his gift passes.

The tale's narrative frame emphasizes the circumstantial limits on art. The narrator remains largely absent during the tale, allowing Copley to make the judgments. But near the opening, the narrator reveals himself a feeling human being: "Captain Hunnewell then took Drowne by the button, and communicated his wishes in so low a tone, that it would be unmannerly to repeat what was evidently intended for the carver's private ear. We shall, therefore, take the opportunity to give the reader a few desirable particulars about Drowne himself" (10:307). With this comment, the narrator becomes a helpless observer of this drama, not its controller. And after drawing the grand conclusions about art and human nature cited earlier, the narrator closes the tale with a paragraph relating a rumor about a woman who stayed in Boston during this period, concluding: "This fair stranger must have been the original of Drowne's Wooden Image" (10:320).

Thus, a tale offering large judgments of art and society, ends not with any of these insights, but with a rumor identifying the person who inspired Drowne's achievement. Even the narrative structure of the tale reminds the reader that art, no matter how noble, grows from and returns to human restraints. The narrator creates a tale that mimics Drowne's ascent to genius and fall back into the mundane.

"The Snow-Image"

Although "The Snow-Image" repeats many ideas from "Drowne's Wooden Image," their new context shifts the emphasis. "The Snow-Image" also presents art as a fusion of invention and fact. In this tale, two imaginative children build a snow maiden with such inspiration she comes to life. Although their ability to dream distinguishes both, the girl, Violet, is the more spiritual and thoughtful of the two and gives orders to her sturdy brother, Peony. He collects the snow needed to fulfill Violet's fantasies. Still, despite their differences, the snow image's loveliness depends on their collaboration: "Now, for a few moments, there was a busy and earnest, but indistinct hum of the two children's voices, as Violet and Peony wrought together with one happy consent. Violet still seemed to be the guiding spirit; while Peony acted rather as a laborer, and brought her the snow from far and near. And yet the little urchin evidently had a proper understanding of the matter, too!" (11:12)[16] The children find their snow creature so beautiful, they kiss her. In response, she runs around the yard with them. As in "Drowne's Wooden Image," the creation's vitality comes from her creator's love for her.

As the titles suggest, "The Snow-Image" and "Drowne's Wooden Image" both portray art as a product of and an emanation from nature. While Drowne's figurehead realizes patterns implicit in its wood, the snow image grows from the snow. The artistic molding of these elements realizes rather than violates their intrinsic nature. Imagination and nature complete and fulfill each other when they collaborate in a work of art.

The strong tie between nature and art receives even more emphasis and development in "The Snow-Image" than in "Drowne's Wooden Image." After the maiden is finished, snow birds settle on her. As she dances about the yard, the neighbors see only a snowdrift pushed around by the wind. The narrator tells us she looks like a star. And when Mr. Lindsey, the children's father, insists the snow child come inside and warm herself, she melts.

The children's pleasure in making the snow maiden and their faith in her ties creativity to human nature. The mother shares their trust, but laughs at her own credulity. The narrator explains that the mother's childlike innocence allows her to understand her children: "All through life, she had kept her heart full of childlike simplicity, and faith, which was as pure and clear as crystal; and, looking at all matters through this transparent medium, she sometimes saw truths so profound, that other people laughed at them as nonsense and absurdity" (11:20). Also, her intense love for her children makes identification with their point of view irresistible. The mother's emotional and imaginative life connects her to the impulses and faith of childhood. In this tale, the instincts and beliefs most abandon as they age naturally culminate in art.

The children's father represents society. As the narrator explains, Mr. Lindsey, like most "excellent" people, is pragmatic, insensitive, and dumb: he was an exceedingly matter-of-fact sort of man, a dealer in hardware, and was sturdily accustomed to take what is called the common-sense view of all matters that came under his consideration. With a heart about as tender as other people's, he had a head as hard and impenetrable, and therefore perhaps as empty, as one of the iron-pots which it was a part of his business to sell. The mother's character, on the other hand, had a strain of poetry in it, a trait of unworldly beauty, a delicate and dewy flower, as it were, that had survived out of her imaginative youth, and still kept itself alive amid the dusty realities of matrimony and motherhood. (11:7)

When Mr. Lindsey comes home from work, proclaims the snow image a real child, and drags her inside to warm up, the mother abandons her point of view and runs to find mittens for the snow maiden. The narrator tells us the mother usually defers to the father; no wonder, since he articulates the point of view society considers mature and reasonable. But the narrator finds Mr. Lindsey's perspective destructive, a judgment certified by the snow maiden's demise and by the contrast between the beautiful descriptions of her dancing outside as the evening sky tries on different light and color combinations and the oppressive Lindsey living room. A hot, black stove stands at the middle, thick red curtains cover the windows, and a heavy smell fills the air: "The difference betwixt the atmosphere here, and the cold, wintry twilight, out of doors, was like stepping at once from Nova Zembla to the hottest part of India, or from the North-pole into an oven. Oh, this was a fine place for the little white stranger!" (11:23).

The room reflects Mr. Lindsey's stolid world. When the snow maiden melts, Mr. Lindsey conveniently forgets her and explains the water as a residue of his children's carelessness. Mr. Lindsey needs his stultifying version of truth too much to admit error. The narrator thinks the tale suggests many morals relevant to Mr. Lindsey's narrowness, but sees no point in proclaiming them because "There is no teaching anything to wise men of good Mr. Lindsey's stamp. They know everything—Oh, to be sure!—everything that has been, and everything that is, and everything that, by any future possibility, can be. And, should some phenomenon of Nature or Providence transcend their system, they will not recognize it, even if it come to pass under their very noses" (11:25).

So "The Snow-Image" repeats many of the notions about art in "Drowne's Wooden Image": both tales present art as a synthesis of fact and imagination that fulfills rather than violates nature, and both link the production and comprehension of art to an individual rather than a conventional perspective. But "The Snow-Image" makes much more explicit than "Drowne's Wooden Image" the hostility between the pragmatic point of view encouraged and reinforced by society and the emotional and imaginative vitality central to art.

"The Snow-Image" also talks repeatedly of benevolence. Mr. Lindsey sees himself as the child's savior and the narrator constantly praises him, calling him "an excellent . . . man" (11:7) and an "honest and very kind-hearted man" (11:19). The irony of these judgments becomes clear when the narrator describes Mr. Lindsey dragging the snow maiden to her death: "And so, with a most benevolent smile on his sagacious visage, all purple as it was with the cold, this very well-meaning gentleman took the snow-child by the hand" (11:21). The ironic descriptions of Lindsey as "kind" and "benevolent" make clear the incompatibility of narrow-mindedness and genuine compassion.

In order to help others, one must understand their perspectives; or, as the narrator puts it: "It behoves men, and especially men of benevolence, to consider well what they are about, and, before acting on their philanthropic purposes, to be quite sure that they comprehend the nature and all the relations of the business in hand. What has been established as an element of good to one being, may prove absolute mischief to another" (11:25). Many critics see this narrative pronouncement as the tale's theme. Indeed, the love, imagination, and hope Lindsey ridicules in his wife and children build bridges between people far more effectively than the conformity and righteousness he espouses. Thus, other critics believe the tale emphasizes society's hostility to art.

But the story also suggests a redemptive role for art. Since the innocent perspective common to Mrs. Lindsey, Violet, and Peony produces the snow maiden, may not art recall people to the empathy and trust they enjoyed as children? May not art reunite people with physical nature and with aspects of their human nature they have abandoned to assume society's point of view? These possibilities become realized only when people, unlike Mr. Lindsey, achieve the humility and courage to let go of convention and risk looking at reality from other angles. Art can help, if they will let it.

So Hawthorne's artists and the scientists undermine their lives and their craft by insisting on illusory control. In "Drowne's Wooden Image" and "The Snow-Image," good art involves renouncing the attempt to impose one's views on the world in order to allow a collaboration between the artist's perceptions, feelings, attachments, and materials.

Using all these dimensions requires the artist to call upon many capacities simultaneously; this exercise generates vitality both in the artist and in the work. "The Snow-Image" suggests this complicated process takes place so naturally that executing it gives enormous pleasure. "Drowne's Wooden Image" adds that people become most themselves when they create. What keeps people from enjoying this innate playfulness? Like Ethan Brand, most people strive for success at the cost of life itself. By definition, artists and scientists see the world differently from most people, but Hawthorne regrets that they too often fall victim to the same emotional limits, the same insistence on rectitude, the same fear of facing their flaws undermining more conventional lives. If people could recover their joy in using all their capacities, they could save their lives. But most prefer the illusion of perfection to vitality's messiness.

Perspective, Humility, and Joy

The issue of perspective rests at the center of all Hawthorne's tales, for his particular stands on individualism, community, art, and science suggest everyone has a limited understanding of truth. Although most people resist accepting their frailties, their shared imperfection unites people, gives life zest by multiplying their views of it, and guarantees them an endless supply of challenges. Although no one can arrive at the truth, everyone can move toward wisdom, and as awareness grows, so does the capacity for love.

"The Hall of Fantasy"

The narrator of "The Hall of Fantasy" tours the building where those dominated by their imaginations gather. He first encounters poets, then businessmen, then inventors, and, finally, reformers. Throughout the story, the narrator tries to establish himself as a realist, but, over and over, he must admit the power of fantasy in all lives, including his.

From the start, he concedes that all people enter the Hall at some point in their lives, if only "by the universal passport of dream" (10:173). Later, he grants that fantasy makes life's sorrows endurable. Through imagination, the convict goes free, the old person reclaims youth, the ill person becomes well, and those who grieve rejoin those they've lost: "It may be said, in truth, that there is but half a life—the meaner and earthlier half—for those who never find their way into the hall" (10:179).

And even though he finds the reformers' schemes unrealistic, allowing their hopes to influence him beautifies society: "In the enthusiasm of such thoughts, I gazed through one of the pictured windows; and, behold! the whole external world was tinged with the dimly glorious aspect that is peculiar to the Hall of Fantasy; insomuch that it seemed practicable, at that very instant, to realize some plan for the perfection of mankind" (10:181). Indeed, dreams give meaning and direction to every human life. Everyone wants the earth to persist and their lives to last so they can strive for their goals. So fantasy pervades public and private life. People retreat to it every night when they sleep, form communities to achieve collective aims, and wake up day after day inspired by the hope of fulfilling some purpose. All human lives rest on and return to dreams; people merely use physical reality to achieve their fantastic schemes.

Yet most human beings present themselves as level-headed and practical. The narrator portrays this conflict between the depth of everyone's commitment to imagination and the universal pretense of hardheadedness. He consistently tries to maintain a pragmatic stance, and just as consistently contradicts himself or discovers his arguments incontrovertibly defeated by the guide leading him through the Hall of Fantasy.

When the narrator meets the poets, he admits to the reader he feels drawn to them, and describes their liveliness and wit, but refuses to admit this attraction to the guide. Instead, he says: "Thank heaven, . . . we have done with this techy, wayward, shy, proud, unreasonable set of laurel-gatherers. I love them in their works, but have little desire to meet them elsewhere." His guide notes the narrator has "adopted an old prejudice" and explains the poets are pleasant, even generous, human beings.

The narrator replies simply, "The world does not think so," revealing why he publicly adopts a view at odds with his personal beliefs: society encourages realism, so he pretends to it, even though it means mouthing dishonest, unkind remarks. The narrator elaborates on this bias: "An author is received in general society pretty much as we honest citizens are in the Hall of Fantasy. We gaze at him as if he had no business among us, and the question whether he is fit for any of our pursuits." The guide replies simply, "Then it is a very foolish question" (10:175–176) and introduces the narrator to the Hall's wild men, the entrepreneurs whose delusions of efficiency lead them to propose ridiculous enterprises, like diverting the sea in order to put down roads. The factual content of these plans disguises their romantic genesis. The guide points out that poets, unlike businessmen, know the difference between reality and fantasy.

When the narrator and his guide come to the reformers, the narrator finds their hopes attractive, but says they need to expose their plans to the sunlight. The seductive, variegated light of the Hall of Fantasy gives them unreasonable optimism. Father Miller's predictions of the world's end especially disturb the narrator. First, he explains he wants the world to exist until it reveals its purpose. The guide counters that if the earth exists to realize some grand design, limited, narrow-minded human beings could not grasp it: "I cannot perceive that our own comprehension of it is at all essential to the matter. At any rate, while our view is so ridiculously narrow and superficial, it would be absurd to argue the continuance of the world from the fact, that it seems to have existed hitherto in vain" (10:182).

The narrator then insists he wants the earth to persist because he has such a strong tie to it. The guide asks why; even if the earth passes away, men's imaginations can and will recreate whatever earthly objects they love: "Standing in this Hall of Fantasy, we perceive what even the earth-clogged intellect of man can do, in creating circumstances, which, though we call them shadowy and visionary, are scarcely more so than those that surround us in actual life. Doubt not, then, that man's disembodied spirit may recreate Time and the World for itself, with all their peculiar enjoyments, should there still be human yearnings amid life eternal and infinite"(10:184). The guide adds that the world seems so chaotic, he can't imagine wanting to recreate it, a point the narrator has also made.

Finally, the narrator leaves the Hall, vowing to return only occasionally because one must live in the real world. So he persists in his illogical realism even though the arguments of his guide, as well as his private reactions, undermine all justification for identifying pragmatism with truth. But, in the last sentence of the story, which most critics believe states the story's theme, the narrator bows to imagination: "Let us be content, therefore, with merely an occasional visit, for the sake of spiritualizing the grossness of this actual life, and prefiguring to ourselves a state, in which the Idea shall be all in all" (10:185). In other words, he sees living in fantasy as the goal of life. One endures actuality while waiting for release into dream.

This story argues that the more openly one acknowledges the role of fantasy in one's life, the saner and more brotherly one becomes. When people deny their dreams, they become absurd, like the inventors who produce "at least fifty kinds of perpetual motion, one of which was applicable to the wits of newspaper editors and writers of every description" (10:178). The schemes of the openly idealistic reformers share a commendable purpose: "Far down, beyond the fathom of the intellect, the soul acknowledged that all these varying and conflicting developments of humanity were united in one sentiment. Be the individual theory as wild as fancy could make it, still the wiser spirit would recognize the struggle of the race after a better and purer life, than had yet been realized on earth" (10:180–181). Although he dismisses their proposals, the reformers' faith moves the narrator.

Kindest of all are the writers, for they embrace fantasy. As a result, they do not take individual perceptions too seriously. They know everyone dreams. The multitude of changing illusions gives pleasure and light, just like the fountain at the center of the Hall, "the water of which continually throws itself into new shapes, and snatches the most diversified hues from the stained atmosphere around. It is impossible to conceive what a strange vivacity is imparted to the scene by the magic dance of this fountain, with its endless transformations, in which the imaginative beholder may discern what form he will" (10:174).

Not surprisingly, the poets drink most often from this fountain, have the least impulse to impose their points of view on others, and have the strongest sense of democracy. This story asserts universal equality: no one understands reality and everyone interprets it through a private dream. The convention of associating truth with materialism makes people dishonest with themselves and suspicious of others, and divides people into camps instead of allowing them to welcome and enjoy the various, incomplete, imperfect views all human beings hold of the world.

"Old News"

"Old News" illustrates how history puts parameters on perception. This tale presents a narrator's reaction to newspapers from three periods, twenty years apart. The newspapers suggest each era has a different mood. Gloom characterizes colonial times: "In vain, we endeavor to throw a sunny and joyous air over our picture of this period; nothing passes before our fancy but a crowd of sad-visaged people, moving duskily through a dull gray atmosphere" (11:135). The narrator describes "The Old French War" in terms of combat and materialism. During the Revolutionary War, he notes both social and personal upheaval and discord. So in a sixty-year period, the tenor of life in the American colonies alters radically, and the minds of its citizenry must shift with the times.

The narrator describes each era differently, in all three cases basing his comments on their newspapers. When discussing colonial times, he attempts to read the papers through the eyes of a colonial merchant, but he can do little more then list the items the tradesman reads. So the narrator drops this approach and launches into his own judgments, citing particulars probably taken from the newspapers. Then he remembers the merchant, returns to him, and imagines what kinds of errands this man would perform, presumably using the names of establishments advertised in the paper. He concludes this section by wondering if the merchant considered his death: "Did he bethink him to call at the workshop of Timothy Sheaffe, in Cold-lane, and select such a grave-stone as would best please him? There wrought the man, whose handi-work, or that of his fellow-craftsmen, was ultimately in demand by all the busy multitude, who have left a record of their earthly toil in these old time-stained papers. And now, as we turn over the volume, we seem to be wandering among the mossy stones of a burial-ground" (11:141). This morbid closing partly reflects the narrator's sense it was an era of suffering, but also suggests his difficulty empathizing with this period, a judgment reinforced by the mechanical way he enters into the colonial merchant's point of view.

In the next section, the narrator sympathizes a bit more, weaving data from the papers with vibrant descriptions. For instance, he talks of how strange it must have looked when merchants gathered at Lake George to sell their wares to the armies: "Carcasses of bullocks and fat porkers are placed upright against the huge trunks of the trees; fowls hang from the lower branches, bobbing against the heads of those beneath." But this period, like the one before, depresses him; further on in this description, the narrator stands back and says: "Imagine such a scene, beneath the dark forest canopy, with here and there a few struggling sunbeams, to dissipate the gloom" (11:148).

He enjoys describing the era's opulence, but he constantly notes that this luxury has long since vanished: "Make way for the phantom-ladies, whose hoops require such breadth of passage, as they pace majestically along, in silken gowns, blue, green, or yellow, brilliantly embroidered, and with small satin hats surmounting their powered hair. Make way; for the whole spectral show will vanish, if your earthly garments brush against their robes" (11:151–152). He considers it appropriate that a fire ends this materialistic era.

The narrator assumes the perspective of a Tory for much of the third section, perhaps as a result of realizing at the end of the second that the more particular and emotional he makes his presentation, the greater its impact: "Did we desire to move the reader's sympathies, on this subject, we would not be grandiloquent about the sea of billowy flame, the glowing and crumbling streets, the broad, black firmament of smoke, and the blast of wind, that sprang up with the conflagration and roared behind it. It would be more effective, to mark out a single family, at the moment when the flames caught upon an angle of their dwelling" (11:152). He identifies with the Tory, allowing him to lead the reader into the Tory's mind. So the narrator recognizes that since history consists of one value scheme replacing another, understanding it means not collecting data, or imagining dramatic scenes, but empathizing with the perspectives dominating each era. The narrator never forgets, in the first section, that the colonists he conjures up have passed away or, in the second, that this environment has vanished. But the Tory moves him.

Besides illustrating the importance of perspective to both enduring and comprehending historical change, this last section raises general issues about point of view. The Tory hangs on to his pre-revolutionary perspective because, as he explains, using a royal "we" that presumably includes the narrator, "Our mind had grown too rigid to change any of its opinions, when the voice of the people demanded, that all should be changed" (11:154). When he goes out into society, he feels ashamed because his attitudes exclude him from conventional patterns; so he is "marked out by a depressed and distrustful mien abroad—as one conscious of a stigma upon his forehead, though for no crime" (11:154). Other citizens punish him for his intransigence with shouts, mud, and dirty water. The Tory's experiences confirm both the arbitrariness and the righteousness of the prevailing point of view.

The narrator loathes the era's smugness and intellectual rigidity: "Almost all our impressions, in regard to this period are unpleasant, whether referring to the state of civil society, or to the character of the contest, which, especially where native Americans were opposed to each other, was waged with the deadly hatred of fraternal enemies. It is the beauty of war, for men to commit mutual havoc with undisturbed good humor" (11:160). In war, societies encourage their citizens to kill in defense of their limited perspectives. If people could hear others' outlooks and own the relativity of theirs, perhaps they would war less.

But most stay trapped in one attitude. As a result, people live most comfortably through ages in which one outlook dominates: "A revolution, or anything, that interrupts social order, may afford opportunities for the individual display of eminent virtue; but, its effects are pernicious to general morality. Most people are so constituted, that they can be virtuous only in a certain routine; and an irregular course of public affairs demoralizes them" (11:159). Still, those aspiring to wisdom and kindness must avoid settling into a single point of view for a lifetime. Even if societies resist tolerance, it benefits the individual to cultivate it. Socially approved views inevitably shift, so it behooves the individual to adjust with them. Otherwise, like the Old Tory, one lives uneasily, waiting for "the impious novelty, that has distracted our latter years, like a wild dream, [to] give place to the blessed quietude of royal sway" (11:154). So "Old News" addresses the issue of point of view on several levels. Since history presents a sequence of shifting perspectives, one best understands it by empathizing with the stance of each era. Moreover, cultivating intellectual flexibility makes people kinder, smarter, and more content.

"The Celestial Rail-road"

In "The Celestial Rail-road," Hawthorne criticizes the assumptions shaping his own age. When the narrator of this story decides to travel to the Celestial City, like Christian in John Bunyan's *The Pilgrim's Progress*, he discovers scientific improvements have made the trip more convenient. The tale recasts Christian's journey to Heaven in terms of values endemic in the nineteenth century.

In Bunyan's book, pilgrims walked to salvation burdened by their sins; the narrator rides a train with a place to store his baggage. Bunyan's pilgrims had to endure ostracism; now, the most fashionable people make the trip. To prevent conflict, modern pilgrims even refrain from discussing religion: "There was much pleasant conversation about the news of the day, topics of business, politics, or the lighter matters of amusement; while religion, though indubitably the main thing at heart, was thrown tastefully into the back-ground" (10: 188–189). So Hawthorne characterizes his contemporaries as obsessed with materialism, indifferent to religious matters, and inclined to assume that improving their physical circumstances magically heals their spiritual lives.

As the new pilgrims travel along routes cleared of danger through the miracle of modern technology, they come to the cave where "two cruel giants, Pope and Pagan," lurked in Bunyan's book. Now the Giant Transcendentalist lives there. Since the Giant Transcendentalist "makes it his business to seize upon honest travellers, and fat them for his table with plentiful meals of smoke, mist, moonshine, raw potatoes, and saw-dust" (10:196–197), Hawthorne dismisses transcendentalism as too insubstantial to redeem his times. Nor does Hawthorne hope conventional religion can save his society. In the shining modern world, the ministers, who have names like Rev. Mr. Shallow-deep and the Rev. Mr. Stumble-at-truth, have moved to Vanity Fair. As a result, people receive a spiritual education with no effort: "Thus literature is etherealized by assuming for its medium the human voice; and knowledge, depositing all its heavier particles— except, doubtless, its gold—becomes exhaled into a sound, which forthwith steals into the ever-open ear of the community. These ingenious methods constitute a sort of machinery, by which thought and study are done to every person's hand, without his putting himself to the slightest inconvenience in the matter" (10:198–199). So transcendentalism and the church give Hawthorne's contemporaries only an illusory spiritual education. Most critics see this as the story's theme.

An author who struggles to handle and present multiple points of view, who favors those characters with the most intellectual flexibility, and who sees humility and acceptance of human frailty as the gateway to wisdom, would not enjoy watching his contemporaries trade their souls for glistening clichés. In this tale, Hawthorne traces spiritual bankruptcy to the obsession with scientific achievements, for these advances give people the delusion of control. Hawthorne reminds his readers that altering physical circumstances cannot cure moral ailments.

The narrator eventually realizes his guide to the Celestial City is the devil, wakes, and discovers he dreamt the trip. But Hawthorne intends this dream to expose the confusion of material and ethical advance he saw condemning his contemporaries to shallow lives. Putting these judgments in someone's dream softens their impact, and the narrator definitely feels relieved when he wakes; but Hawthorne believed dreams, fantasies, and even tales often expose inconvenient truths excluded from the conventional order. That the narrator must dream his way into his spiritual life emphasizes the narrowness strangling his time.

"Sights from a Steeple"

"Sights from a Steeple" elaborates on Hawthorne's reservations about transcendentalism. The narrator begins by explaining he has climbed a steeple in hope of entering and enjoying heaven. But as he approaches his goal, he feels ambivalent about it. He loves the idea of celestial escape, but shivers at the isolation this release involves. His vacillating descriptions of the clouds reflect his confusion: sometimes they invite him, other times they threaten him. He concludes by emphatically asserting ambivalence: "Every one of those little clouds has been dipped and steeped in radiance, which the slightest pressure might disengage in silvery profusion, like water wrung from a sea-maid's hair. Bright they are as a young man's visions, and, like them, would be realized in chilliness, obscurity and tears. I will look on them no more" (9:192).

He turns his attention to the earth below, three-quarters of it occupied by people. But he stands too far above his fellow mortals to see into their lives: "O that the Limping Devil of Le Sage would perch beside me here, extend his wand over this contiguity of roofs, uncover every chamber, and make me familiar with their inhabitants! The most desirable mode of existence might be that of a spiritualized Paul Pry, hovering invisible round man and woman, witnessing their deeds, searching into their hearts, borrowing brightness from their felicity, and shade from their sorrow, and retaining no emotion peculiar to himself. But none of these things are possible" (9:192).

So the narrator contents himself with recording the human activity he can see. He describes people walking down the street, sometimes guessing their intentions, but primarily reporting the obvious. He senses his account lacks significance and promises that insights well up in him, but they never appear. So he teeters on the brink of an idea, then talks about the weather: "There are broad thoughts struggling in my mind, and, were I able to give them distinctness, they would make their way in eloquence. Lo! the rain-drops are descending" (9:196).

The narrator cannot grasp the purposes of the humanity he observes, so he cannot give his story substance. The rainstorm dictates the tale's narrative movement. Since his perch in the clouds gives him a good view of the storm, his account of the rain's impact has a specificity, vitality, and direction that his comments about human beings lack: "The large drops descend with force upon the slated roofs, and rise again in smoke. There is a rush and roar, as of a river through the air, and muddy streams bubble majestically along the pavement, whirl their dusky foam into the kennel, and disappear beneath iron grates." But his closeness to the storm irritates him: "I love not my station here aloft, in the midst of the tumult which I am powerless to direct or quell, with the blue lightning wrinkling on my brow, and the thunder muttering its first awful syllables in my ear" (9:197–198). He recognizes he has elevated himself into an alien natural order. He pledges to return to the human order.

But the tale hints that returning to society will not take the narrator home. When he observes the people below, he notes little positive about their lives. He guesses those working on the dock would like to leave, and those hiding in their houses suffer from guilt. He describes marching soldiers encountering a funeral and, finally, sees human beings below as victimized by the storm as he. His observations offer no hope that he'll enjoy himself once he descends.

Not surprisingly, the narrator turns back to the sky as it promises to burst with sunshine. He appears to resolve his ambivalence by riding this sunshine to a higher reality: "A little speck of azure has widened in the western heavens; the sunbeams find a passage, and go rejoicing through the tempest; and on yonder darkest cloud, born, like hallowed hopes, of the glory of another world, and the trouble and tears of this, brightens forth the Rainbow!" (9:198). He opened the tale with similar longing: "O that I could soar up into the very zenith, where man never breathed, nor eagle ever flew, and where the ethereal azure melts away from the eye, and appears only a deepened shade of nothingness!" (9:191). The tale demonstrates where this goal takes him. Why would identification with nature prove humanly satisfying? Nature will always remain beyond human influence, so it can provide only temporary relief, not enduring consolation. The narrator's fantasy of escaping into nature means leaving an admittedly imperfect human world to enter the void.

The tale seems a clear attack on transcendentalists who condemn the materialism of most people's lives, and offer as an alternative a spiritual sublimity achieved by withdrawing from social influences and resigning to nature. The identification with nature Emerson and Thoreau favored looks empty, cold, and simplistic in this tale.

The narrator's distance from others robs him and his reflections of substance. Detachment, whether scientific or spiritual, destroys significance. Human interaction creates meaning. This narrator can record human events and guess at a multitude of purposes, but because he has no connection to what he observes, he can discover no import in it. The tale acquires its significance from the reader's experience of the randomness, vacuity, and circularity of the narrator's musings. Similarly, the narrator of "The Celestial Rail-road" brings a narrowly physical understanding of reality to Bunyan's book. He, too, lives in a meaningless world. So these tales suggest that the detachment of both the scientific and the transcendental stance breeds emptiness.

"Sylph Etherege"

"Sylph Etherege" juxtaposes the intellectual, materialistic, arrogant bias Hawthorne again and again associates with his age and with science to a gentler, more imaginative attitude resembling that of the transcendentalists. Sylph Etherege represents the imaginative position. Orphaned when young and raised by a bachelor uncle, Sylph has few human ties to connect her to this world, so she retreats into a fanciful one she can fill with companions. She especially enjoys weaving fantasies around the cousin to whom she was betrothed when young, Edgar Vaughan. Her uncle dies, Sylph becomes the ward of Mrs. Grosvenor, "a lady of wealth and fashion" (11:113), and waits to marry Edgar, literally, the man of her dreams.

Edgar decides Sylph has spun too ornate a fantasy for him to match, so he poses as his closest friend, Edward Hamilton, and sets out to cure Sylph of her illusions. He gives Sylph a miniature he represents as Edgar Vaughan; in fact, the picture reflects and reinforces Sylph's fantasy lover. And, as Edgar anticipated, Sylph retreats further into her dream world.

Edgar expects that when he identifies himself, Sylph will recognize the futility of her illusions and accept reality. Mrs. Grosvenor plays along because she likes Edgar and hopes he is right, but she occasionally doubts their plan; her uneasiness proves appropriate.

When Edgar tells Sylph the truth, she faints. As they are about to marry, Sylph looks more ethereal than ever: "Vaughan was already attentively observing his mistress, who sat in a shadowy and moonlighted recess of the room, with her dreamy eyes fixed steadfastly upon his own. The bough of a tree was waving before the window, and sometimes enveloped her in the gloom of its shadow, into which she seemed to vanish." Vaughan comments that she looks as if "she will fade into the moonlight" or "flit away upon the breeze." Although Sylph denies she will do either, she says farewell and vows: "You cannot keep me here!" As the story ends, Mrs. Grosvenor rushes toward Sylph to save her, and Edgar says: " 'Stay!' cried he, with a strange smile of mockery and anguish. 'Can our sweet Sylph be going to Heaven, to seek the original of the miniature?' " (11:118–119). The story ends here.

Edgar's attempt to tame Sylph's imagination fails; it may even kill her. Why does he try? Because he fears Sylph's dreams establish expectations he cannot meet, so he teaches her to count on nothing but cruelty from him. From the tale's beginning, Edgar appears well-bred, intelligent, and controlling: "His features wore even an ominous, though somewhat mirthful expression, while he pointed his long forefinger at the girl, and seemed to regard her as a creature completely within the scope of his influence" (11:111). This story makes little distinction between dominating someone's judgment and devouring someone's soul. Condemning your fiancée to spending her life with a dishonest and manipulative spouse dooms her to humiliation and uncertainty. No wonder as the tale proceeds, Vaughan looks increasingly menacing; his smile, an "expression of mockery and malice" (11:114), grown more prominent. When he approaches Sylph with the truth, his smile consumes his face and establishes his contrast to her miniature.

Sylph's fantasies come from her soul. She hoped to find in her lover a resonance with and reinforcement of her own point of view: "She heard the melody of a voice breathing sentiments with which her own chimed in like music. Oh, happy, yet hapless girl! Thus to create the being whom she loves, to endow him with all the attributes that were most fascinating to her heart, and then to flit with the airy creature into the realm of fantasy and moonlight, where dwelt his dreamy kindred!" (11:115–116). The narrator, like Edgar Vaughan, sees Sylph's absorption in illusion as problematic, but taking away all possibility of finding sympathy in this world does not reconcile Sylph to actuality. Vaughan uses his insight to undermine Sylph's point of view; she responds by clinging to fantasy more desperately because his brutality makes reality all the more threatening.

The tale criticizes both an intellectual, calculating approach to reality and an idealistic, imaginative one. It further suggests people do not change their points of view when threatened with domination by another. Moreover, to subvert someone else's worldview and substitute one's own, amounts to psychic murder.

Sadly, the potential existed for their differences to enrich Edgar and Sylph's lives. The letters between them establish a bond: "For several years, a correspondence had been kept up between the cousins, and had produced an intellectual intimacy, though it could but imperfectly acquaint them with each other's character" (11:112). Self-righteousness transforms a protentially educative relationship into a destructive one. Vaughan's refusal to allow Sylph's perspective to influence him pushes her away, and Sylph's refusal to accept the limits of reality pushes her from the world. Edgar's aggression makes him the larger villain, but if both had more empathy, they might have solved their conflict constructively. True wisdom consists not in asserting the rightness of one's perspective but in cultivating the humility to understand other points of view.

Vaughan's civilized veneer and Mrs. Grosvenor's popularity identify their attitudes as more characteristic of their society than Sylph's. Thus, the tale offers a glimpse of what will happen to relationships if people adopt the scientist's objective, rational, controlling point of view. Like Aylmer, Vaughan observes, understands, and manipulates Sylph in a manner certifying his intellect and his cruelty. If, like Mrs. Grosvenor, the rest of the world puts aside its innate sense of moral appropriateness in deference to cultivated intelligence, imagination and vulnerability may vanish into the moonlight like Sylph.

"Rappaccini's Daughter"

"Rappaccini's Daughter" describes another clash in perspective, this time between the detached intellectual knowledge of the scientist and the emotional knowledge love produces. The tale sides with love, but warns that our world may be too corrupt to nurture and learn from tenderness.

As the tale opens, Giovanni Guasconti has come to study at the University of Padua. The room where he stays overlooks a garden full of unusual plants. Their artificiality makes some of them frightening, as if "the production was no longer of God's making, but the monstrous offspring of man's depraved fancy, glowing with only an evil mockery of beauty" (10:110).

This garden is the laboratory of Dr. Rappaccini, a sickly-looking scientist whose plants seem to threaten him: "It was strangely frightful to the young man's imagination, to see this air of insecurity in a person cultivating a garden, that most simple and innocent of human toils, and which had been alike the joy and labor of the unfallen parents of the race. Was this garden, then, the Eden of the present world?—and this man, with such a perception of harm in what his own hands caused to grow, was he the Adam?" (10:96). These questions frame the tale, inviting the reader to see it as a parable about the ways people have alienated themselves from nature and each other.

When Rappaccini must touch a flower, he calls on his daughter, Beatrice. She has an intimacy with the plants he lacks; so, unlike Rappaccini, she can handle them without harm. Beatrice resembles the most beautiful, exotic, and poisonous plant in the garden; she even calls it her sister.

67

When Giovanni observes Beatrice from a distance, she frightens him. She appears toxic: flowers wither in her hand; lizards and insects die when exposed to her breath. But when he meets her, the purity of her heart overwhelms him. Giovanni dismisses or rationalizes his earlier fears and believes Beatrice only good.

Baglioni, a friend of Giovanni's parents, and a scientific rival of Rappaccini's, warns Giovanni that Rappaccini plots against him. When Baglioni calls on Giovanni, he notes an odor in the room, suggesting it comes from Beatrice who, like the plant she calls her sister, may be toxic. Baglioni gives Giovanni an antidote and hope of curing Beatrice. When Giovanni prepares to visit Beatrice with the cure, he notices flowers withering in his hands. Beatrice has poisoned him.

When he confronts her with this discovery, Beatrice reprimands him, reminding him she has a pure heart. She takes the antidote, but the narrator reports that Giovanni's angry words have destroyed their relationship. Beatrice must seek refuge in another world: "Oh, weak, and selfish, and unworthy spirit, that could dream of an earthly union and earthly happiness as possible, after such deep love had been so bitterly wronged as was Beatrice's love by Giovanni's blighting words! No, no; there could be no such hope. She must pass heavily, with that broken heart, across the borders of Time—she must bathe her hurts in some fount of Paradise, and forget her grief in the light of immortality—and *there* be well!" (10:126). Beatrice drinks the remedy and dies, blaming her father for his interference and Giovanni for his cruelty.

Her accusations bewilder her father, who thinks his experiment not only guaranteed her a lifelong companion, but also saved her from remaining "a weak woman, exposed to all evil, and capable of none." Beatrice replies that she "would fain have been loved, not feared," but her father understands only power.

Baglioni resurfaces at the end of the story to blame Rappaccini: "And is *this* the upshot of your experiment?" (10:127–128). Baglioni conveniently forgets he supplied the antitoxin that kills Beatrice, just as he neglects to tell Giovanni that his objections to Rappaccini result not from suspicions of Rappaccini's scientific ability, but from professional jealousy. Since Beatrice's death would help certify Baglioni's superiority to Rappaccini, he may well have orchestrated it.

Baglioni and Rappaccini lack compassion, and both struggle to dominate others. Beatrice operates out of love and acceptance. Giovanni wavers between these two stances, sometimes embracing one, sometimes embracing the other, sometimes caught in ambivalence. The narrator favors Beatrice even though she has a fatal blindness: she watches things die when she breathes on them and crosses herself; she pulls herself away from Giovanni for fear her touch may harm him; but it never occurs to her, her breath may poison him as it does insects and lizards. Beatrice's toxicity presents a genuine problem, and her ignorance of it suggests willful ignorance. Still, the narrator proclaims repeatedly, if Giovanni had more depth, he would join Beatrice's point of view:

> There is something truer and more real, than what we can see with the eyes, and touch with the finger. On such better evidence, had Giovanni founded his confidence in Beatrice, though rather by the necessary force of her high attributes, than by any deep and generous faith, on his part. But, now, his spirit was incapable of sustaining itself at the height to which the early enthusiasm of passion had exalted it; he fell down, grovelling among earthly doubts, and defiled therewith the pure whiteness of Beatrice's image. (10:120)

It seems strange the narrator favors a character so out of touch with reality, who, pure heart notwithstanding, condemns Giovanni to what she describes as "an awful doom" (10:123). Also, the difference between Beatrice's solution and Sylph Etherege's seems slight. These difficulties have caused some commentators to call the narrator unreliable. As Carol Bensick explains: "The narrator expects Giovanni to believe like a convert while remaining in the condition of the natural man. . . . Hawthorne's tale as a whole shows that Transcendental romantic idealism cannot be used as a guide for actual historical experience."[17]

Perhaps the narrator leaves Beatrice's redemptive qualities undeveloped to invite the reader to accept her goodness on faith. For those so corrupted by the modern world that they need more evidence to consider Beatrice an angel, passages from Hawthorne's earlier tale "The New Adam and Eve" help explain the narrator's affection for Beatrice's loving blindness. "The New Adam and Eve" traces in imagination the probable consequences if all people disappeared and Adam and Eve started over. When Adam examines some books, the narrator hopes he will leave them alone and avoid "all the perversions and sophistries, and false wisdom so aptly mimicking the true; all the narrow truth, so partial that it becomes more deceptive than falsehood; all the wrong principles and worse practice, the pernicious examples and mistaken rules of life" (10:265). So this tale, like "Rappaccini's Daughter," condemns intellectual knowledge as incomplete and dangerous in large part because it presents itself as true.

When Adam and Eve wander into an empty jail, the narrator comments that it housed people who bore the burden for everyone's flaws: "Feeling its [sin's] symptoms within the breast, men concealed it with fear and shame, and were only the more cruel to those unfortunates whose pestiferous sores were flagrant to the common eye" (10:254). The jail's existence shows how people tried everything to cure sin except what works: love. The narrator urges Adam and Eve to leave prison before they too become infected with sin, deny it, and project it on others. Again, like "Rappaccini's Daughter," this tale condemns the common tendency to blame everyone else for evil.

Adam and Eve do move on, and by the end of the story their love for each other and their natural religious faith give them an optimism and happiness that will endure no matter what happens. Even if they die that evening, they know, as Adam says: "Another morn will find us somewhere beneath the smile of God." Eve adds: "And no matter where we exist . . . we shall always be together" (10:267). Beatrice also contends that only love and faith matter. Giovanni worries about externals. Beatrice's inadvertent injury to his body turns his love to hate and his religious faith to scorn. He sarcastically asks her to kiss him: "Let us join our lips in one kiss of unutterable hatred, and so die!" Beatrice responds with a prayer to the Virgin, and Giovanni declares her beyond redemption: "'Thou! Dost thou pray?' cried Giovanni, still with the same fiendish scorn. 'Thy very prayers, as they come from thy lips, taint the atmosphere with death'" (10:124).

Other Hawthorne tales illuminate Beatrice's childlike innocence. In "Little Annie's Ramble," the narrator refreshes his soul by wandering with a little girl: "After drinking from those fountains of still fresh existence, we shall return into the crowd, as I do now, to struggle onward and do our part in life, perhaps as fervently as ever, but, for a time, with a kinder and purer heart, and a spirit more lightly wise. All this by thy sweet magic, dear little Annie!" (9:129).

The image of drinking water from the fountain also appears in "Rappaccini's Daughter." The narrator sometimes connects these refreshing images to Beatrice: "Her spirit gushed out before him like a fresh rill, that was just catching its first glimpse of the sunlight, and wondering at the reflections of earth and sky which were flung into its bosom. There came thoughts, too, from a deep source, and fantasies of a gemlike brilliancy, as if diamonds and rubies sparkled upward among the bubbles of the fountain" (10:113).

The water that nourishes the garden symbolizes the nature that persists and remains true to itself despite the way different cultures use it; the water seems "an immortal spirit, that sung its song unceasingly, and without heeding the vicissitudes around it; while one century embodied it in marble, and another scattered the perishable garniture on the soil" (10:94–95).

In "A Rill from the Town Pump," the pump expresses the same idea, adding that human beings would do well to mimic the calm, ever adaptable mode of nature: "In the moral warfare, which you are to wage—and, indeed, in the whole conduct of your lives—you cannot choose a better example than myself, who have never permitted the dust, and sultry atmosphere, the turbulence and manifold disquietudes of the world around me, to reach that deep, calm well of purity, which may be called my soul. And whenever I pour out that soul, it is to cool earth's fever or cleanse its stains" (9:147–148). The only character in "Rappaccini's Daughter" with a cool, accepting soul is Beatrice. To sustain her serenity, she must leave a world of people intent on dominating each other in the name of one limited truth or another.

"Rappaccini's Daughter" needs illumination with other tales because it focuses on the human tragedy created by intellectual arrogance, merely hinting at the solution Beatrice offers. Critics, naturally enough, tend to mimic the characters of the tale, debating who deserves the blame for Beatrice's death. Rappaccini's scientific arrogance receives the most frequent condemnation. Another sizable number of commentators fault Giovanni's shallowness, while others condemn Baglioni as well as Rappaccini and Giovanni. A few add Beatrice to this list of villains. The merit of all these accusations confirms Beverly Haviland's judgment: "By provoking us to disagree with each other about what the story means, about what its sources are, about whether it is allegory at all, Hawthorne has produced a critical discourse in which differences must be preserved because there is no possibility of agreement. . . . One celebrates the continuity of life, its temporality, by keeping in mind that truths are many, not one. Accepting ambivalence and disagreement as inevitable, perhaps one is then fit to be a member of the audience Hawthorne imagined."[18]

"The May-pole of Merry Mount"

"The May-pole of Merry Mount" develops Beatrice's stance more fully. The tale describes a historical moment when two perspectives clash by portraying a conflict between two groups, the Merry Mounters and the Puritans, each dominated by an extreme point of view. The Merry Mounters, who have fled the growing influence of the Puritan sobriety in England, believe only in mirth. They construct a society where everyone strives to have fun; they even have merry funerals. The central symbol of their culture is the Maypole because "May, or her mirthful spirit, dwelt all the year round at Merry Mount" (9:54).

Since the Merry Mounters never reflect, they renounce the capacity Hawthorne believes distinguishes men from beasts. Correspondingly, some Merry Mounters wear stag's antlers or goat's horns, while others dance with a bear whose "inferior nature rose half-way, to meet his companions as they stooped" (9:56).

The Merry Mounters' attitude seems appropriate to childhood. Defending this carelessness from life's unavoidable lessons in pain and death requires dishonesty: "The elder spirits, if they knew that mirth was but the counterfeit of happiness, yet followed the false shadow wilfully, because at least her garment glittered brightest. Sworn triflers of a lifetime, they would not venture among the sober truths of life, not even to be truly blest" (9:59–60).

As determinedly gloomy and pessimistic as the Merry Mounters are happy, the Puritans spend their time praying and working, keeping guns handy to shoot savages: "Their festivals were fast-days, and their chief pastime the singing of psalms" (9:61). The Puritan equivalent of the Maypole is the whipping post.

The Puritans and their pessimism inevitably conquer the Merry Mount world, "as the moral gloom of the world overpowers all systematic gaiety" (9:66). Most critics agree the tale slightly favors the Puritan perspective. Caught in this transition are two newlyweds from Merry Mount, Edith and Edgar. Since they have spent their lives at Merry Mount, they know about mirth. But as they marry, each experiences sadness: "No sooner had their hearts glowed with real passion, then they were sensible of something vague and unsubstantial in their former pleasures, and felt a dreary presentiment of inevitable change. From the moment that they truly loved, they had subjected themselves to earth's doom of care, and sorrow, and troubled joy, and had no more a home at Merry Mount" (9:58). When they feel love, they begin to take life seriously, guaranteeing pain. Caring about another human being makes laughing at funerals difficult.

Edith and Edgar have allowed their minds and their emotions to grow with their lives. The midsummer roses crowning and surrounding them confirm the naturalness of this development: "Bright roses glowed in contrast with the dark and glossy curls of each, and were scattered round their feet, or had sprung up spontaneously there" (9:56–57).

When the Puritans arrive on the scene, Endicott threatens the Merry Mounters with brandings, stripes, and imprisonments, ordering his men to shoot the bear to prevent it from practicing witchcraft. As he approaches Edith and Edgar, each asks for the other's punishment. Their love moves even Endicott, who recognizes that their seriousness could make them valuable Puritans. He assures Edith and Edgar they will find more joy toiling for the Puritan community than dancing around a Maypole. Then he crowns them with roses. The narrator tells the readers Endicott is correct. Although Edith and Edgar never return to Merry Mount, "As their flowery garland was wreathed of the brightest roses that had grown there, so, in the tie that united them, were intertwined all the purest and best of their early joys. They went heavenward, supporting each other along the difficult path which it was their lot to tread, and never wasted one regretful thought on the vanities of Merry Mount" (9:67).

Both Puritans and Merry Mounters recognize Edith and Edgar have a naturalness others lack. A number of critics agree with this judgment. The ability to accept and integrate the changes in their surroundings and in their emotions not only distinguishes them, it allows them to adjust to their new situation and develop as human beings.

Since life inevitably brings confrontations between perspectives, those who do not merely submit to the "truths" promulgated around them, but instead listen to and develop a point of view from their own responses and experiences, will come closer to seeing all of reality and find it easier to adjust to change. Moreover, sensitivity and loyalty to feeling, as well as flexibility, rest at the heart of good relationships. These people not only move with the times more agilely than most, they love more fervently.

"The Great Carbuncle"

In "The Great Carbuncle," Hawthorne once again links wisdom, versatility, and love. In this tale, several people gather to search the mountains for a legendary bright stone called the Great Carbuncle. Most of the searchers' motivations reflect their obsessions. For instance, Mr. Pigsnort, the businessman, will sell it to the highest bidder; the poet will observe it to inspire his poetry; the scientist will analyze it to establish his reputation; the aristocrat will use it to illuminate his ancestral home. But the most absurd characters are the Seeker and the Cynic.

The Seeker has devoted his life to finding the stone, vowing that if he discovers it, he will drag it into a cave and die. The Cynic pursues the Great Carbuncle to prove it does not exist. A pair of newlyweds, Matthew and Hannah, have several modest goals. They hope it will light up their cabin, making it easier to find things like needles; they believe their neighbors would enjoy looking at it, and think they would like having enough light in their home to see each other's faces in the middle of the night.

While the others smile at the couple's simplicity, Matthew and Hannah's plans have a complexity the others' lack; they offer pragmatic, aesthetic, social, and personal reasons for wanting the Carbuncle.

In the morning, Matthew and Hannah wake to find their obsessive campmates gone. They follow as quickly as possible, supporting each other both physically and emotionally. Finally, they reach the Carbuncle. Two of the other searchers have preceded them. The Seeker stands dead with his arms outstretched toward the rock; his singular purpose fulfilled, he has no reason to live. The Cynic claims he sees nothing. Irritated by the Cynic's perversity, Matthew tells him to take off his glasses. The Cynic does, the Carbuncle's light blinds him, and he sees nothing, ever.

Matthew and Hannah take a look at the Carbuncle and pronounce it too bright for their lives. The same naturalness and adaptability that make their goals more complex than the other searchers', allow Hannah and Matthew to renounce the stone. Matthew vows, "Never again will we desire more light than all the world may share with us" (9:163). The narrator agrees their affection has more value than otherworldly sublimity: "She and her husband fell asleep with hands tenderly clasped, and awoke, from visions of unearthly radiance, to meet the more blessed light of one another's eyes" (9:158). Many critics see this as the tale's theme. The tale reinforces the Carbuncle's unnaturalness by placing it above the timberline, in a desolate landscape where nothing flourishes. Matthew and Hannah know accepting their humanity brings them deeper joy than transcendence.

The other searchers continue in their ruts. Finding the Carbuncle would have merely contributed another incident to their predictable lives. The scientist's analysis of granite brings him as much fame as the Carbuncle would have; the poet writes about a piece of ice that answers to his conception of the Carbuncle. The tale does not relate the futures of Matthew and Hannah, nor does it need to. This couple's flexibility, humility, compassion, and love guarantee a lifetime of intellectual and emotional riches.

"The Great Stone Face"

Newlyweds offer an obvious example of affection, but Hawthorne by no means limits love to the recently married. In "The Ambitious Guest," he presents an affectionate family, and in "The Great Stone Face," he characterizes a loving individual.

The Great Stone Face is a natural rock formation that overlooks the valley below like a serene, benevolent deity. The people regularly exposed to it say one day a person will appear who shares the Great Stone Face's sublimity. No one cherishes this hope more than Ernest, who studies the kindly face from childhood. The narrator attributes Ernest's absorption in the Great Stone Face to his goodness:

> When the toil of the day was over, he would gaze at it for hours, until he began to imagine that those vast features recognized him, and gave him a smile of kindness and encouragement, responsive to his own look of veneration. We must not take upon us to affirm that this was a mistake, although the Face may have looked no more kindly at Ernest than at all the world besides. But the secret was, that the boy's tender and confiding simplicity discerned what other people could not see; and thus the love, which was meant for all, became his peculiar portion. (11:29)

Over the years, the people think various men from the valley fulfill the prophecy, but to Ernest their faces reveal their failure to realize the values exemplified by The Great Stone Face. The first candidate, Mr. Gathergold, has spent his life collecting money; he has an appropriately "tight" face: he has "skin as yellow as if his own Midas-hand had transmuted it" and "a low forehead, small, sharp eyes, puckered about with innumerable wrinkles, and very thin lips, which he made still thinner by pressing them forcibly together" (11:32). The next candidate, Old Blood-and-Thunder, surprises Ernest; he expected the person resembling the Great Stone Face to be a man of peace, not war, but Ernest hopes he errs. Unfortunately, he is correct: "He beheld a war-worn and weather-beaten countenance, full of energy, and expressive of an iron will; but the gentle wisdom, the deep, broad, tender sympathies, were altogether wanting" (11:37).

The third candidate, a politician and lawyer, Old Stony Phiz, has the right features, but his face lacks hope and depth: he "had always a weary gloom in the deep caverns of his eyes, as of a child that has outgrown its playthings, or a man of mighty faculties and little aims, whose life, with all its high performances, was vague and empty, because no high purpose had endowed it with reality" (11:41).

All these candidates reflect the tendency to confuse the appearance of greatness with the reality. Gathergold's riches represent the highest accomplishment in a materialistic society. When his stature dissolves along with his wealth, the villagers move on to Old Blood-and Thunder, someone distinguished by the ability to defeat others. Finally, they select a politician noted for winning arguments; again, someone who dominates. All three demonstrate an ability to control. Although many characters in Hawthorne's fiction confuse power with greatness, only those with the humility to cultivate acceptance of nature, themselves, and others actually achieve it.

Ernest himself discovers someone he thinks may measure up, a poet whose work captures some of the kindness and sublimity of the Great Stone Face. His poetry, like the art Hawthorne characterizes favorably in "Drowne's Wooden Image" and "The Snow-Image," grows from, expresses, and realizes nature: "Thus the world assumed another and a better aspect from the hour that the poet blessed it with his happy eyes. The Creator had bestowed him, as the last, best touch to his own handiwork. Creation was not finished till the poet came to interpret, and so complete it."

The poet sees and records the same goodness in human beings: "He showed the golden links of the great chain that intertwined them with an angelic kindred." He visits Ernest and they enjoy rich talk: "The sympathies of these two men instructed them with a profounder sense than either could have attained alone. Their minds accorded into one strain, and made delightful music which neither of them could have claimed as all his own, nor distinguished his own share from the other's" (11:43–45). So it disappoints and surprises Ernest to see that the poet does not resemble the Great Stone Face. The poet explains that even though he has generous thoughts, he cannot sustain this hopefulness, nor does it govern his conduct.

While candidates come and go, Ernest matures into a kinder, wiser person. People from all around value his simple, profound talk: "Whether it were sage, statesman, or philanthropist, Ernest received these visitors with the gentle sincerity that had characterized him from boyhood, and spoke freely with them of whatever came uppermost, or lay deepest in his heart or their own" (11:42). Eventually, he starts giving sermons in an appropriately natural setting: "Set in a rich frame-work of verdure, there appeared a niche, spacious enough to admit a human figure, with freedom for such gestures as spontaneously accompany earnest thought and genuine emotion." The consistency of Ernest's words, thoughts, and actions give them force: "His words had power, because they accorded with his thoughts, and his thoughts had reality and depth, because they harmonized with the life which he had always lived" (11:47).

The poet goes to watch Ernest preach, and as Ernest stops to reflect, the poet notices his face "assumed a grandeur of expression, so imbued with benevolence," that the poet announces Ernest fulfills the prophecy. The others present agree, but Ernest hopes "some wiser and better man than himself would by-and-by appear, bearing a resemblance to the GREAT STONE FACE" (11:48). Ernest preserves the humility explaining and nurturing his magnanimity. As many critics note, his willingness to resign his ego to the influence of the face, to the influence of nature, to the influence of those he encounters makes Ernest good and wise. His inability to declare himself great guarantees his benevolence and insight will continue to grow.

"The Great Stone Face" reviews false claims of control that surface in one Hawthorne tale after another, reemphasizing that money, power, and fame all pass away. Artists able to resign themselves to nature may produce something sublime, but true genius belongs to those with the faith to trust nature, themselves, and others so completely that this optimism pervades their thoughts, their speech, and their behavior. Despite the error and cruelty recorded in other tales, this one implies the world struggles toward benevolence. Even an image of kindness makes people reach for goodness. Cultivating this faith means renouncing pride and the hopeless enterprise of attempting to redeem one's life by striving for superiority. If people cultivate and live in terms of their humane impulses, they will find not only integrity, but also wisdom.

"The Haunted Mind"

Although Hawthorne's tales suggest human beings have internal monitors capable of guiding them toward full, happy lives, most of his characters have more difficulty heeding theirs than Ernest. "The

Haunted Mind" provides a paradigm of the convoluted route most of Hawthorne's characters must take to peace.

The narrator wakes in the middle of the night and sees it as a chance to explore the contemplative mode central to Hawthorne's tales: "Yesterday has already vanished among the shadows of the past; to-morrow has not yet emerged from the future. You have found an intermediate space, where the business of life does not intrude; where the passing moment lingers, and becomes truly the present; a spot where Father Time, when he thinks nobody is watching him, sits down by the way side to take breath" (9:305).

In this state, the outside world looks cold; lying in bed, engaged by one's thoughts, seems attractive. But eventually this self-absorption sets loose failed hopes, evil deeds, and missed chances. Coldness settles on the heart: "This nightmare of the soul; this heavy, heavy sinking of the spirits; this wintry gloom about the heart; this indistinct horror of the mind, blending itself with the darkness of the chamber" (9:307). The narrator turns toward the world for relief, dissipating his sadness by focusing on objects around his room. But genuine calm comes only when he imagines a woman in bed with him. Facing faults makes him seek companionship: "Throughout the chamber, there is the same obscurity as before, but not the same gloom within your breast. As your head falls back upon the pillow, you think—in a whisper be it spoken—how pleasant in these night solitudes, would be the rise and fall of a softer breathing than your own, the slight pressure of a tenderer bosom, the quiet throb of a purer heart, imparting its peacefulness to your troubled one, as if the fond sleeper were involving you in her dream" (9:308).

Then the narrator moves on to expansive and joyous images. The journey through guilt to love allows him to enjoy life with Whitmanesque enthusiasm: "You sink down in a flowery spot, on the borders of sleep and wakefulness, while your thoughts rise before you in pictures, all disconnected, yet all assimilated by a pervading gladsomeness and beauty" (9:308).

In the closing paragraph, the narrator develops "a doubtful parallel between human life and the hour which has now elapsed. In both you emerge from mystery, pass through a vicissitude that you can but imperfectly control, and are borne onward to another mystery" (9:309). This "doubtful parallel" captures the central psychological process in Hawthorne's fiction. His best characters acknowledge that they can only "imperfectly control" what happens and realize that living means progressing from mystery to mystery. Their humility allows them to seek the company of others, and, warmed by sympathy, confusions change from threats to opportunities.

Even in the somber context of "The Haunted Mind," Hawthorne ties this happy state to childhood and nature. The narrator's concluding elation begins with these images: "The wheeling of gorgeous squadrons, that glitter in the sun, is succeeded by the merriment of children round the door of a school-house, beneath the glimmering shadow of old trees, at the corner of a rustic lane" (9:308). And, indeed, both children and nature travel from mystery to mystery with beauty and grace. Hawthorne sees maintaining this joyous spirit while facing life's inevitable sorrows as the greatest human achievement.

For only faith can allow human beings to own and learn from sadness, and lack of it drives people to false optimism. Those who embrace either convention or individualism enjoy a shallow certitude at odds with both reality and their own nature. Those who aspire to perfect control cultivate an illusion dangerous to both themselves and others. Those who resist acknowledging and moving beyond the inevitable limits of their points of view choose stagnation and delusion. Still, most attempt to hide in these falsehoods from imperfection and uncertainty. Hawthorne's tales not only expose these evasions, they show how accepting, not disowning, frailty brings both individual fulfillment and profound connections to others. Nothing explains and illustrates the intellectual, aesthetic, moral, and emotional rewards of humility, flexibility, and courage more tellingly than Hawthorne's short fiction.

Notes to Part 1

1. William Charvat, Roy Harvey Pearce, Claude M. Simpson, Fredson Bowers, Matthew Bruccoli, L. Neal Smith, John Manning, J. Donald Crowley, Thomas Woodson, Bill Ellis, James A. Rubino, James Kayes, Edward H. Davidson, eds., *The Centenary Edition of the Works of Nathaniel Hawthorne*, 20 Vols. (Columbus, Ohio: Ohio State University Press, 1962–1988); hereinafter noted parenthetically with the volume number followed by the page number.

2. *The Writings of Nathaniel Hawthorne* (Boston and New York: Houghton, Mifflin and Company, 1900), 17:402–403.

3. Arlin Turner, ed., *Hawthorne as Editor: Selections from his Writings in the American Magazine* (Baton Rouge, La.: Louisiana State University Press, 1941), 210.

4. "Hawthorne Revisited: Some Remarks on Hellfiredness," *Sewanee Review* 81 (1973): 93.

5. Critics taking this view include Seymour Gross in "Hawthorne's 'Lady Eleanore's Mantle' as History," *Journal of English and German Philology* 54 (October 1955): 553, and Julian Smith in "Hawthorne's 'Legends of the Province House,'" *Nineteenth Century Fiction* 24 (June 1969): 37.

6. "The Oft-Told *Twice-Told Tales*: Their Folklore Motifs," *Southern Folklore Quarterly* 22 (June 1958): 73.

7. Sheila Dwight argues there is an unpardonable sin in "Hawthorne and the Unpardonable Sin," *Studies in the Novel* 2 (1970): 449–458.

8. "The Head, the Heart, and the Unpardonable Sin," *New England Quarterly* 40 (March 1967): 46.

9. "The Villagers and 'Ethan Brand,'" *Studies in Short Fiction* 4 (1967): 262.

10. Lawrence Scanlon has also noted similarities between the narrator and Heidegger in "That Very Singular Man, Dr. Heidegger," *Nineteenth Century Fiction* 17 (December 1962): 253–263.

11. "A Fearful Power: Hawthorne's View on Art and the Artist as Expressed in his Sketches and Short Stories," *Nathaniel Hawthorne Journal* 8 (1978): 134.

12. *The Pursuit of Form: A Study of Hawthorne and the Romance* (Urbana, Illinois: University of Illinois Press, 1970), 60.

13. Other critics noting the narrator's ambivalence include Patricia Moyer in "Time and the Artist in Kafka and Hawthorne," *Modern Fiction Studies* 4 (Winter 1958–1959): 301, and Thomas Walsh in "Hawthorne's Handling of Point of View in his Tales and Sketches," unpublished dissertation (University of Wisconsin, 1957), 334.

14. "Hawthorne's Tale Told Twice: A Reading of 'Wakefield,'" *ESQ* 28 (1982): 230.

15. "The Enchanted Ground: An Approach to the Tales and Sketches of

Nathaniel Hawthorne," unpublished dissertation (Columbia University, 1966), 135.

16. Darrel Abel also makes this point in "The Theme of Isolation in Hawthorne," *Personalist*, 32 (1951): 188.

17. *La Nouvelle Beatrice: Renaissance and Romance in "Rappaccini's Daughter"* (New Brunswick, N.J.: Rutgers University Press, 1985), 122–123.

18. "The Sin of Synecdoche: Hawthorne's Allegory Against Symbolism in 'Rappaccini's Daughter,'" *Texas Studies in Literature and Language* 29 (1987): 297.

Part 2

THE WRITER

Nathaniel Hawthorne's suspicion of general judgments helps explain his limited and scattered comments on writing. He comes closest to broad analysis in the brief prefaces introducing his works. So, the first section, "The Prefaces," collects samples from Hawthorne's prefaces to his short story collections. These introductions present a more relaxed persona than the reader of Hawthorne's best-known tales would anticipate. But, despite the amiable surface, they assert a link between solitary reflection and universal truth explicable only in terms of an intuitive knowledge of and faith in the unconscious. The preface to "Mosses from an Old Manse" ties the world of Hawthorne's short stories to dream. The others talk of his limited audience and his isolation, implying that the solitude feeding his tales gives him access to the "universal heart," and exposes his readers to a shared psychology obscured by more conventional means of asserting brotherhood.

Hawthorne believed when he wrote most honestly from his own depths, he spoke most tellingly to and for others. He understood many would have difficulty hearing him, but apparently had more faith in youngsters than adults, for he offers the children constituting his audience for *The Wonder Book* no explanations before leaping into fable. But their elders need coaxing from the reassuringly genial author to put their common sense aside and enter into fantasy.

The second section, "Principles and Procedures," presents Hawthorne's views about writing primarily through excerpts from his notebooks and letters. The notebook entries show how his tales grew from ideas. The first two quotations present the germs of "The Great Stone Face" and "The Birth-mark," while the third sets out the central psychological pattern of Hawthorne's short stories. The comments taken from his letters establish Hawthorne's commitment to integrity as well as his understanding that although one cannot write well without remaining loyal to one's perspective, because all human beings have limited points of view, integrity does not guarantee wisdom.

The third section, "The Struggle to Write and Live," shows Hawthorne's battle to reconcile the solitude that fed his writing with his psychic and financial need to move into the world. As the letter to Longfellow shows, Hawthorne hoped leaving his chamber would improve his work. But his subsequent letters to Sophia Peabody, his future wife, make it clear ordinary work obstructed his writing. He turned to Sophia as a muse who would protect and nurture the spiritual life sustaining his fiction while he set his sensibilities aside to earn a living. As these selections demonstrate, Hawthorne successfully alternated between writing and more lucrative employment until he accepted the appointment as counsel to Liverpool. His comments suggest that job brought him too thoroughly into the real world for him to fully recover his imaginative life.

The Prefaces

From the Preface to
Mosses from an Old Manse

When summer was dead and buried, the old Manse became as lonely as a hermitage. Not that ever—in my time, at least—it had been thronged with company; but, at no rare intervals, we welcomed some friend out of the dusty glare and tumult of the world, and rejoiced to share with him the transparent obscurity that was flung over us. In one respect, our precincts were like the Enchanted Ground, through which the pilgrim travelled on his way to the Celestial City. The guests, each and all, felt a slumberous influence upon them; they fell asleep in chairs, or took a more deliberate siesta on the sofa, or were seen stretched among the shadows of the orchard, looking up dreamily through the boughs. They could not have paid a more acceptable compliment to my abode, nor to my own qualities as a host. I held it as a proof, that they left their cares behind them, as they passed between the stone gate-posts, at the entrance of our avenue; and that the so powerful opiate was the abundance of peace and quiet, within and all around us. Others could give them pleasure and amusement, or instruction—these could be picked up anywhere—but it was for me to give them rest—rest, in a life of trouble. What better could be done for those weary and world-worn spirits?—for him, whose career of perpetual action was impeded and harassed by the rarest of his powers, and the richest of his acquirements?—for another, who had thrown his ardent heart, from earliest youth, into the strife of politics, and now, perchance, began to suspect that one lifetime is too brief for the accomplishment of any lofty aim?—for her, on whose feminine nature had been imposed the heavy gift of intellectual power, such as a strong man might have staggered under, and with it the necessity to act upon the world?—in a word, not to multiply instances, what better could be done for anybody, who came within our magic circle, than to throw the spell of a tranquil spirit over him? And when it had wrought its full effect, then we dismissed him, with but misty reminiscences, as if he had been dreaming of us.

Were I to adopt a pet idea, as so many people do, and fondle it in my embraces to the exclusion of all others, it would be, that the great want which mankind labors under, at this present period, is—sleep! The world should recline its vast head on the first convenient pillow, and take an age-long nap. It has gone distracted, through a morbid activity, and, while preternaturally wide-awake, is nevertheless tormented by visions, that seem real to it now, but would assume their true aspect and character, were all things once set right by an interval of sound repose. This is the only method of getting rid of old delusions, and avoiding new ones—of regenerating our race, so that it might in due time awake, as an infant out of dewy slumber—of restoring to us the simple perception of what is right, and the single-hearted desire to achieve it; both of which have long been lost, in consequence of this weary activity of brain, and torpor or passion of the heart, that now afflicts the universe. Stimulants, the only mode of treatment hitherto attempted, cannot quell the disease; they do but heighten the delirium.

And now, I begin to feel—and perhaps should have sooner felt—that we have talked enough of the old Manse. Mine honored reader, it may be, will vilify the poor author as an egotist, for babbling through so many pages about a moss-grown country parsonage, and his life within its walls, and on the river, and in the woods,—and the influences that wrought upon him, from all these sources. My conscience, however, does not reproach me with betraying anything too sacredly individual to be revealed by a human spirit, to its brother or sister spirit. How narrow— how shallow and scanty too—is the stream of thought that has been flowing from my pen, compared with the broad tide of dim emotions, ideas, and associations, which swell around me from that portion of my existence! How little have I told!—and, of that little, how almost nothing is even tinctured with any quality that makes it exclusively my own! Has the reader gone wandering, hand in hand with me, through the inner passages of my being, and have we groped together into all its chambers, and examined their treasures or their rubbish? Not so. We have been standing on the green sward, but just within the cavern's mouth, where the common sunshine is free to penetrate, and where every footstep is therefore free to come. I have appealed to no sentiment or sensibilities, save such as are diffused among us all. So far as I am a man of really individual attributes, I veil my face; nor am I, nor have ever been, one of those supremely hospitable people, who serve up their own hearts delicately fried, with brain-sauce, as a tidbit for their beloved public.

Glancing back over what I have written, it seems but the scattered reminiscences of a single summer. In fairy-land, there is no measurement of time; and, in a spot so sheltered from the turmoil of life's ocean, three years hastened away with a noiseless flight, as the breezy sunshine chases the cloud-shadows across the depths of a still valley.

The Preface to *Twice-Told Tales*

The author of TWICE-TOLD TALES has a claim to one distinction, which, as none of his literary brethren will care about disputing it with him, he need not be afraid to mention. He was, for a good many years, the obscurest man of letters in America.

These stories were published in Magazines and Annuals, extending over a period of ten or twelve years, and comprising the whole of the writer's young manhood, without making (so far as he has ever been aware) the slightest impression on the Public. One or two among them— "The Rill from the Town-Pump" in perhaps a greater degree than any other—had a pretty wide newspaper-circulation; as for the rest, he has no grounds for supposing, that, on their first appearance, they met with the good or evil fortune to be read by anybody. Throughout the time above-specified, he had no incitement to literary effort in a reasonable prospect of reputation or profit; nothing but the pleasure itself of composition—an enjoyment not at all amiss in its way, and perhaps essential to the merit of the work in hand, but which, in the long run, will hardly keep the chill out of a writer's heart, or the numbness out of his fingers. To this total lack of sympathy, at the age when his mind would naturally have been most effervescent, the Public owe it, (and it is certainly an effect not to be regretted, on either part,) that the Author can show nothing for the thought and industry of that portion of his life, save the forty sketches, or thereabouts, included in these volumes.

Much more, indeed, he wrote; and some very small part of it might yet be rummaged out (but it would not be worth the trouble) among the dingy pages of fifteen-or-twenty-year-old periodicals, or within the shabby morocco-covers of faded Souvenirs. The remainder of the works, alluded to, had a very brief existence, but, on the score of brilliancy, enjoyed a fate vastly superior to that of their brotherhood, which succeeded in getting through the press. In a word, the Author burned them without mercy or remorse, (and, moreover, without any subsequent

"Preface" to *Twice-Told Tales*, *The Centenary Edition*, 9:3–7. Copyright 1974 by Ohio State University Press. Reprinted with permission.

regret,) and had more than one occasion to marvel that such very dull stuff, as he knew his condemned manuscripts to be, should yet have possessed inflammability enough to set the chimney on fire!

After a long while, the first collected volume of the Tales was published. By this time, if the Author had ever been greatly tormented by literary ambition, (which he does not remember or believe to have been the case,) it must have perished, beyond resuscitation, in the dearth of nutriment. This was fortunate; for the success of the volume was not such as would have gratified a craving desire for notoriety. A moderate edition was "got rid of" (to use the Publisher's very significant phrase) within a reasonable time, but apparently without rendering the writer or his productions much more generally known than before. The great bulk of the reading Public probably ignored the book altogether. A few persons read it, and liked it better than it deserved. At an interval of three or four years, the second volume was published, and encountered much the same sort of kindly, but calm, and very limited reception. The circulation of the two volumes was chiefly confined to New England; nor was it until long after this period, if it even yet be the case, that the Author could regard himself as addressing the American Public, or, indeed, any Public at all. He was merely writing to his known or unknown friends.

As he glances over these long-forgotten pages, and considers his way of life, while composing them, the Author can very clearly discern why all this was so. After so many sober years, he would have reason to be ashamed if he could not criticise his own work as fairly as another man's; and—though it is little his business, and perhaps still less his interest—he can hardly resist a temptation to achieve something of the sort. If writers were allowed to do so, and would perform the task with perfect sincerity and unreserve, their opinions of their own productions would often be more valuable and instructive than the works themselves.

At all events, there can be no harm in the Author's remarking, that he rather wonders how the TWICE-TOLD TALES should have gained what vogue they did, than that it was so little and so gradual. They have the pale tint of flowers that blossomed in too retired a shade—the coolness of a meditative habit, which diffuses itself through the feeling and observation of every sketch. Instead of passion, there is sentiment; and, even in what purport to be pictures of actual life, we have allegory, not always so warmly dressed in its habiliments of flesh and blood, as to be taken into the reader's mind without a shiver. Whether from lack of power, or an unconquerable reserve, the Author's touches have often an effect of tameness; the merriest man can hardly contrive to laugh at his broadest humor; the tenderest woman, one would suppose, will hardly shed warm tears at his deepest pathos. The book, if you would see anything in it, requires to be read in the clear, brown, twilight atmosphere in which it was written; if opened in the sunshine, it is apt to look exceedingly like a volume of blank pages.

With the foregoing characteristics, proper to the productions of a person in retirement, (which happened to be the Author's category, at the time,) the book is devoid of others that we should quite as naturally look for. The sketches are not, it is hardly necessary to say, profound; but it is rather more remarkable that they so seldom, if ever, show any design on the writer's part to make them so. They have none of the abstruseness of idea, or obscurity of expression, which mark the written communications of a solitary mind with itself. They never need translation. It is, in fact, the style of a man of society. Every sentence, so far as it embodies thought or sensibility, may be understood and felt by anybody, who will give himself the trouble to read it, and will take up the book in a proper mood.

This statement of apparently opposite peculiarities leads us to a perception of what the sketches truly are. They are not the talk of a secluded man with his own mind and heart, (had it been so, they could hardly have failed to be more deeply and permanently valuable,) but his attempts, and very imperfectly successful ones, to open an intercourse with the world.

The Author would regret to be understood as speaking sourly or querulously of the slight mark, made by his earlier literary efforts, on the Public at large. It is so far the contrary, that he has been moved to write this preface, chiefly as affording him an opportunity to express how much enjoyment he has owed to these volumes, both before and since their publication. They are the memorials of very tranquil and not unhappy years. They failed, it is true—nor could it have been otherwise—in winning an extensive popularity. Occasionally, however, when he deemed them entirely forgotten, a paragraph or an article, from a native or foreign critic, would gratify his instincts of authorship with unexpected praise;—too generous praise, indeed, and too little alloyed with censure, which, therefore, he learned the better to inflict upon himself. And, by-the-by, it is a very suspicious symptom of a deficiency of the popular element in a book, when it calls forth no harsh criticism. This has been particularly the fortune of the TWICE-TOLD TALES. They made no enemies, and were so little known and talked about, that those who read, and chanced to like them, were apt to conceive the sort of kindness for the book, which a person naturally feels for a discovery of his own.

This kindly feeling, (in some cases, at least,) extended to the Author, who, on the internal evidence of his sketches, came to be regarded as a mild, shy, gentle, melancholic, exceedingly sensitive, and not very forcible man, hiding his blushes under an assumed name, the quaintness of which was supposed, somehow or other, to symbolize his personal and literary traits. He is by no means certain, that some of his subsequent productions have not been influenced and modified by a natural desire to fill up so amiable an outline, and to act in consonance with the character assigned to him; nor, even now, could he forfeit it without a few tears of tender sensibility. To conclude, however;—these volumes have opened the way to most agreeable associations, and to the formation of imperishable friendships; and there are many golden threads, interwoven with his present happiness, which he can follow up more or less directly, until he finds their commencement here; so that his pleasant pathway among realities seems to proceed out of the Dream-Land of his youth, and to be bordered with just enough of its shadowy foliage to shelter him from the heat of the day. He is therefore satisfied with what the TWICE-TOLD TALES have done for him, and feels it to be far better than fame.

LENOX, January 11, 1851.

From the Preface to *A Wonder Book*

The author has long been of opinion, that many of the classical myths were capable of being rendered into very capital reading for children. In the little volume here offered to the Public, he has worked up half-a-dozen of them, with this end in view.

In performing this pleasant task—for it has been really a task fit for hot weather, and one of the most agreeable, of a literary kind, which he ever undertook—the Author has not always thought it necessary to write downward, in order to meet the comprehension of children. He has generally suffered the theme to soar, whenever such was its tendency, and when he himself was buoyant enough to follow without an effort. Children possess an unestimated sensibility to whatever is deep or high, in imagination or feeling, so long as it is simple, likewise. It is only the artificial and the complex that bewilders them.

Excerpted from the "Preface" to *A Wonder Book*, *The Centenary Edition* 7:3–4. Copyright 1972 by the Ohio State University Press. Reprinted with permission.

Preface to *The Snow-Image*

To Horatio Bridge, Esq., U. S. N.

MY DEAR BRIDGE:

Some of the more crabbed of my critics, I understand, have pronounced your friend egotistical, indiscreet, and even impertinent, on account of the Prefaces and Introductions with which, on several occasions, he has seen fit to pave the reader's way into the interior edifice of a book. In the justice of this censure I do not exactly concur, for the reasons, on the one hand, that the public generally has negatived the idea of undue freedom on the author's part, by evincing, it seems to me, rather more interest in these aforesaid Introductions than in the stories which followed,—and that, on the other hand, with whatever appearance of confidential intimacy, I have been especially careful to make no disclosures respecting myself which the most indifferent observer might not have been acquainted with, and which I was not perfectly willing that my worst enemy should know. I might further justify myself, on the plea that, ever since my youth, I have been addressing a very limited circle of friendly readers, without much danger of being overheard by the public at large; and that the habits thus acquired might pardonably continue, although strangers may have begun to mingle with my audience.

But the charge, I am bold to say, is not a reasonable one, in any view which we can fairly take of it. There is no harm, but, on the contrary, good, in arraying some of the ordinary facts of life in a slightly idealized and artistic guise. I have taken facts which relate to myself, because they chance to be nearest at hand, and likewise are my own property. And, as for egotism, a person, who has been burrowing, to his utmost ability, into the depths of our common nature, for the purposes of psychological romance,—and who pursues his researches in that dusky region, as he needs must, as well by the tact of sympathy as by the light of observation,—will smile at incurring such an imputation in virtue of a little preliminary talk about his external habits, his abode, his casual associates, and other matters entirely upon the surface. These things hide the man, instead of displaying him. You must make quite another kind of inquest, and look through the whole range of his fictitious characters, good and evil, in order to detect any of his essential traits.

Be all this as it may, there can be no question as to the propriety of my inscribing this volume of earlier and later sketches to you, and pausing here, a few moments, to speak of them, as friend speaks to friend; still being cautious, however, that the public and the critics shall overhear nothing which we care about concealing. On you, if on no other person, I am entitled to rely, to sustain the position of my Dedicatee. If anybody is responsible for my being at this day an author, it is yourself. I know not whence your faith came; but, while we were lads together at a country college,—gathering blue-berries, in study-hours, under those tall academic pines; or watching the great logs, as they tumbled along the current of the Androscoggin; or shooting pigeons and gray squirrels in the woods; or bat-fowling in the summer twilight; or catching trouts in that shadowy little stream which, I suppose, is still wandering riverward through the forest,—though you and I will never cast a line in it again,—two idle lads, in short (as we need not fear to acknowledge now), doing a hundred things that the Faculty never heard of, or else it had been the worse for us,—still it was your prognostic of your friend's destiny, that he was to be a writer of fiction.

And a fiction-monger, in due season, he became. But, was there ever such a weary delay in obtaining the slightest recognition from the public, as in my case? I sat down by the wayside of life, like a man under enchantment, and a shrubbery sprang up around me, and the bushes grew to be saplings, and the saplings became trees, until no exit appeared possible, through the entangling depths of my obscurity. And there, perhaps, I should be sitting at this moment, with the moss on the imprisoning tree-trunks, and the yellow leaves of more than a score of autumns piled above me, if it had not been for you. For it was through your interposition,—and that, moreover, unknown to himself,—that your early friend was brought before the public, somewhat more prominently than theretofore, in the first volume of Twice-told Tales. Not a publisher in America, I presume, would have thought well enough of my forgotten or never noticed stories, to risk the expense of print and paper; nor do I say this with any purpose of casting odium on the respectable fraternity of book-sellers, for their blindness to my wonderful merit. To confess the truth, I doubted of the public recognition quite as much as they could do. So much the more generous was your confidence; and knowing, as I do, that it was founded on old friendship rather than cold criticism, I value it only the more for that.

So, now, when I turn back upon my path, lighted by a transitory gleam of public favor, to pick up a few articles which were left out of my former collections, I take pleasure in making them the memorial of our very long and unbroken connection. Some of these sketches were among the earliest that I wrote, and, after lying for years in manuscript, they at last skulked into the Annuals or Magazines, and have hidden themselves there ever since. Others were the productions of a later period; others, again, were written recently. The comparison of these various trifles— the indices of intellectual condition at far separated epochs—affects me with a singular complexity of regrets. I am disposed to quarrel with the earlier sketches, both because a mature judgment discerns so many faults, and still more because they come so nearly up to the standard of the best that I can achieve now. The ripened autumnal fruit tastes but little better than the early windfalls. It would, indeed, be mortifying to believe that the summertime of life has passed away, without any greater progress and improvement than is indicated here. But,—at least, so I would fain hope,—these things are scarcely to be depended upon, as measures of the intellectual and moral man. In youth, men are apt to write more wisely than they really know or feel; and the remainder of life may be not idly spent in realizing and convincing themselves of the wisdom which they uttered long ago. The truth that was only in the fancy then may have since become a substance in the mind and heart.

I have nothing further, I think, to say; unless it be that the public need not dread my again trespassing on its kindness, with any more of these musty and mouse-nibbled leaves of old periodicals, transformed, by the magic arts of my friendly publishers, into a new book. These are the last. Or, if a few still remain, they are either such as no paternal partiality could induce the author to think worth preserving, or else they have got into some very dark and dusty hiding-place, quite out of my own remembrance and whence no researches can avail to unearth them. So there let them rest.

Very sincerely yours,

N. H.

Lenox, November 1st, 1851.

Principles and Procedures

From *The American Notebooks*

The semblance of a human face to be formed on the side of a mountain, or in the fracture of a small stone, by a *lusus naturæ*. The face is an object of curiosity for years or centuries, and by and by a boy is born, whose features gradually assume the aspect of that portrait. At some critical juncture, the resemblance is found to be perfect. A prophecy may be connected.

A person to be the death of his beloved in trying to raise her to more than mortal perfection; yet this should be a comfort to him for having aimed so highly and holily.

*   *   *

The human Heart to be allegorized as a cavern; at the entrance there is sunshine, and flowers growing about it. You step within, but a short distance, and begin to find yourself surrounded with a terrible gloom, and monsters of divers kinds; it seems like Hell itself. You are bewildered, and wander long without hope. At last a light strikes upon you. You press towards it yon, and find yourself in a region that seems, in some sort, to reproduce the flowers and sunny beauty of the entrance, but all perfect. These are the depths of the heart, or of human nature, bright and peaceful; the gloom and terror may lie deep; but deeper still is this eternal beauty.

Excerpted from *The American Notebooks, The Centenary Edition* 8:184. Copyright 1972 by the Ohio State University Press. Reprinted with permission.
Excerpted from *The American Notebooks, The Centenary Edition* 8:237. Copyright 1972 by the Ohio State University Press. Reprinted with permission.

From a Letter to E. A. Duyckinck
(27 April 1851)

I am glad you think my style plain.[1] I never, in any one page or paragraph, aimed at making it anything else, or giving it any other merit—and I wish people would leave off talking about its beauty. If it have any, it is only pardonable as being unintentional. The greatest possible merit of style is, of course, to make the mere words absolutely disappear into the thought.

Excerpted from a letter to E. A. Duyckinck, *The Centenary Edition* 16:421. Copyright 1985 by Ohio State University Press. Reprinted with permission.

From *The American Notebooks*

. . . these originals in a small way, after one has seen a few of them, become more dull and common-place than even those who keep the ordinary pathway of life. They have a rule and a routine, which they follow with as little variety as other people do *their* rule and routine; and when once we have fathomed their mystery, nothing can be more . . . wearisome. An innate perception and reflection of truth gives the only sort of originality that does not finally grow intolerable.

From *The American Notebooks, The Centenary Edition* 8:357–358. Copyright 1972 by the Ohio State University Press. Reprinted by permission.

From a Letter to L. W. Mansfield (20 February 1850)

If we were sitting together by an evening fireside, and you had imparted the poem to me in your own voice and cadences, and with your own explanatory talk; then—aided, too, by a perception of the poet's own character—I might get light enough upon the matter to throw some of it back from another point of view. Only in such circumstances, I think, can a man be justified in interfering with the process of creation. The requisite of such preliminary criticism is, to have the deepest and warmest sympathy that can co-exist between two perfectly independent perceptions.

Excerpt from a letter to L. W. Mansfield, *The Centenary Edition* 16:319–320. Copyright 1985 the Ohio State University Press. Reprinted with permission.

From *Our Old Home*

At any rate, it must be a remarkably true man who can keep his own elevated conception of truth when the lower feeling of a multitude is assailing his natural sympathies, and who can speak out frankly the best that there is in him, when, by adulterating it a little, or a good deal, he knows that he may make it ten times as acceptable to the audience.

Excerpt from *Our Old Home, The Centenary Edition* 5:330. Copyright 1970 by the Ohio State University Press. Reprinted with permission.

From a letter to Delia Bacon
(24 October 1856)

[Hawthorne paid for the publication of Delia Bacon's book, *The Philosophy of the Plays of Shakespeare Unfolded*, but was not astounded by its disastrous sales and reviews. Hawthorne helped Delia Bacon publish her work because he believed, as he wrote in the introduction, "The volume now before the reader, . . . is the product of a most faithful and conscientious labor, and a truly heroic devotion of intellect and heart. No man or woman has ever thought or written more sincerely than the author of this book."[2] Still, Delia Bacon could not trust him and wrote to him of her uneasiness. This is his reply.]

. . . when people misunderstand me, I seldom take the trouble (and never should, on my own account) to attempt to set them right. I meant, when I began this scrawl, to say something in my own defence; but I find it makes me sick to think of it—so we will let it pass. By telling me what was the state of affairs between yourself and your brother, you made it my duty to give you the best advice I could; and, on further reflection, I find my opinion precisely the same as it was at first. And, seeing with his eyes, I cannot wonder at his acting as he has.

My opinion of the book has never varied; nor have I, up to this moment, spared any effort to bring it before the public, nor relinquished any hope of doing so.

I suppose it would be in vain to tell you that I have never thought, for an instant, of any miserable little interest that I might have, in the success of the book, or in your being on sisterly terms with your brother. But really I don't think you construe me very generously.

However, you will find me always just the same as I have been; and if ever I seem otherwise, the fault is in the eyes that look at me. Nor do I pretend to be very good; there are hundreds of kinder and better people in the world; but such as I am, I am genuine, and in keeping with myself. And, in honest truth, my dear Miss Bacon, I wish to do you what good I can.

Excerpt from a letter to Delia Bacon, *The Centenary Edition* 17:565. Copyright 1987 by the Ohio State University Press. Reprinted with permission.

From a letter to Sophia Peabody (1 May 1841)

Every day of my life makes me feel more and more how seldom a fact is accurately stated; how, almost invariably, when a story has passed through the mind of a third person, it becomes, so far as regards the impression that it makes in further repetitions, little better than a falsehood, and this, too, though the narrator be the most truth-seeking person in existence. How marvellous the tendency is! . . . Is truth a fantasy which we are to pursue forever and never grasp? . . .

Excerpt from a letter to Sophia Peabody, *The Centenary Edition* 15:538. Copyright 1984 by the Ohio State University Press. Reprinted by permission.

From *Our Old Home*

Facts, as we really find them, whatever poetry they may involve, are covered with a stony excrescence of prose, resembling the crust on a beautiful sea-shell, and they never show their most delicate and divinest colors, until we shall have dissolved away their grosser actualities by steeping them long in a powerful menstruum of thought. And, seeking to actualize them again, we do but renew the crust. If this were otherwise—if the moral sublimity of a great fact depended in any degree on its garb of external circumstances, things which change and decay—it could not itself be immortal and ubiquitous, and only a brief point of time and a little neighborhood would be spiritually nourished by its grandeur and beauty.

Excerpt from *Our Old Home, The Centenary Edition* 5:135-136. Copyright 1970 by the Ohio State University Press. Reprinted with permission.

From a Letter to Robert J. Poney
(28 September 1863)

. . . you attribute to me a superiority which I do not dream of asserting. A reader, who can fully understand and appreciate a work, possesses all the faculties of the writer who produced it—except a knack of expression, by which the latter is enabled to give definite shape to an idea or sentiment which he and his appreciative reader possess in common. Thus the advantage on the author's part is but a slight one, and the more truth and wisdom he writes, the smaller is his individual share in it.

The Struggle to Write and Live

From a Letter to Sam M. Cleveland
(8 January 1863)

It may not be amiss to add that I have never applied myself to writing when I have had anything else to do—not having the faculty of literary composition except with a mind wholly unoccupied by other labor.

From a Letter to H. W. Longfellow
(4 June 1837)

Not to burthen you with my correspondence, I have delayed a rejoinder to your very kind and cordial letter, until now. It gratifies me to find that you have occasionally felt an interest in my situation; but your quotation from Jean Paul, about the 'lark-nest,' makes me smile. You would have been much nearer the truth, if you had pictured me as dwelling in an owl's nest; for mine is about as dismal, and, like the owl, I seldom venture abroad till after dusk. By some witchcraft or other—for I really cannot assign any reasonable why and wherefore—I have been carried apart from the main current of life, and find it impossible to get back again. Since we last met—which, I remember, was in Sawtell's room, where you read a farewell poem to the relics of the class—ever since that time, I have secluded myself from society; and yet I never meant any such thing, nor dreamed what sort of life I was going to lead. I have made a captive of myself and put me into a dungeon; and now I cannot find the key to let myself out—and if the door were open, I should be almost afraid to come out. You tell me that you have met with troubles and changes. I know not what they may have been; but I can assure you that trouble is the next best thing to enjoyment, and that there is no fate in this world so horrible as to have no share in either its joys or sorrows. For the last ten years, I have not lived, but only dreamed about living. It may be true that there have been some unsubstantial pleasures here in the shade, which I should have missed in the sunshine; but you cannot conceive how utterly devoid of satisfaction all my retrospects are. I have laid up no treasure of pleasant remembrances, against old age; but there is some comfort in thinking that my future years can hardly fail to be more varied, and therefore more tolerable, than the past.

You give me more credit than I deserve, in supposing that I have led a studious life. I have, indeed, turned over a good many books, but in so desultory a way that it cannot be called study, nor has it left me the fruits of study. As to my literary efforts, I do not think much of them—neither is it worth while to be ashamed of them. They would have been better, I trust, if written under more favorable circumstances. I have had no external excitement—no consciousness that the public would like what I wrote, nor much hope nor a very passionate desire that they should do so. Nevertheless, having nothing else to be ambitious of, I have felt considerably interested in literature; and if my writings had made any decided impression, I should probably have been stimulated to greater exertions; but there has been no warmth of approbation, so that I have always written with benumbed fingers. I have another great difficulty, in the lack of materials; for I have seen so little of the world, that I have nothing but thin air to concoct my stories of, and it is not easy to give a lifelike semblance to such shadowy stuff. Sometimes, through a peep-hole, I have caught a glimpse of the real world; and the two or three articles, in which I have portrayed such glimpses, please me better than the others.

From a Letter to Sophia Peabody
(6 March 1839)

My dear Sophie, your letters are no small portion of my spiritual food, and help to keep my soul alive, when otherwise it might languish unto death, or else become hardened and earth-incrusted, as seems to be the case with almost all the souls with whom I am in daily intercourse. They never interfere with my worldly business—neither the reading nor the answering them—(I am speaking of your letters, not of those "earth-incrusted" souls)—for I keep them to be the treasure of my still and secret hours, such hours as pious people spend in prayer; and the communion which my spirit then holds with yours has something of religion in it. The charm of your letters does not depend upon their intellectual value, though that is great, but on the spirit of which they are the utterance, and which is a spirit of wonderful efficacy. No one, whom you would deem worthy of your friendship, could enjoy so large a share of it as I do, without feeling the influence of your character throughout his own—purifying his aims and desires, enabling him to realize that there is a truer world than this feverish one around us, and teaching him how to gain daily entrance into that better world.

Excerpt from a letter to Sophia Peabody, *The Centenary Edition*, 15:291. Copyright 1984 by Ohio State University Press. Reprinted with permission.

From a Letter to Sophia Peabody
(26 March 1840)

Blessedest, I do think that it is the doom laid upon me, of murdering so many of the brightest hours of the day at that unblest Custom-House, that makes such havoc with my wits; for here I am again, trying to write worthily to my etherealest, and intellectualest, and feelingest, and imaginativest wife, yet with a sense as if all the noblest part of man had been left out of my composition—or had decayed out of it, since my nature was given to my own keeping. Sweetest Dove, shouldst thou once venture within those precincts, the atmosphere would immediately be fatal to thee—thy wings would cease to flutter in a moment—scarcely wouldst thou have time to nestle into thy husband's bosom, ere thy pure spirit would leave what is mortal of thee there, and flit away to Heaven. Never comes any bird of Paradise into that dismal region. A salt, or even a coal ship is ten million times preferable; for there the sky is above me, and the fresh breeze around me, and my thoughts, having hardly anything to do with my occupation, are as free as air.

From a Letter to Cornelius Mathews and Evert A. Duyckinck (22 December 1841)

I do not believe that I shall ever write any more—at least, not like my past productions; for they grew out of the quietude and seclusion of my former life; and there is little probability that I shall ever be so quiet and secluded again. During the last three or four years, the world has sucked me within its vortex; and I could not get back to my solitude again, even if I would.

From a Letter to Sophia Peabody
(4 October 1840)

Here sits thy husband in his old accustomed chamber, where he used to sit in years gone by, before his soul became acquainted with thine. Here I have written many tales—many that have been burned to ashes—many that doubtless deserved the same fate. This deserves to be called a haunted chamber; for thousands upon thousands of visions have appeared to me in it; and some few of them have become visible to the world. If ever I should have a biographer, he ought to make great mention of this chamber of my memoirs, because so much of my lonely youth was wasted here; and here my mind and character were formed; and here I have been glad and hopeful, and here I have been despondent; and here I sat a long, long time, waiting patiently for the world to know me, and sometimes wondering why it did not know me sooner, or whether it would ever know me at all—at least, till I were in my grave. And sometimes (for I had no wife then to keep my heart warm) it seemed as if I were already in the grave, with only life enough to be chilled and benumbed. But oftener I was happy—at least, as happy as I then knew how to be, or was aware of the possibility of being. By and bye, the world found me out in my lonely chamber, and called me forth—not, indeed, with a loud roar of acclamation, but rather with a still, small voice,[3] and forth I went, but found nothing in the world that I thought preferable to my old solitude, till at length a certain Dove was revealed to me, in the shadow of a seclusion as deep as my own had been. And I drew nearer and nearer to the Dove, and opened my bosom to her, and she flitted into it, and closed her wings there—and there she nestles now and forever, keeping my heart warm, and renewing my life with her own. So now I begin to understand why I was imprisoned so many years in this lonely chamber, and why I could never break through the viewless bolts and bars; for if I had sooner made my escape into the world, I should have grown hard and rough, and been covered with earthly dust, and my heart would have become callous by rude encounters with the multitude; so that I should have been all unfit to shelter a heavenly Dove in my arms. But living in solitude till the fulness of time was come, I still kept the dew of my youth and the freshness of my heart, and had these to offer to my Dove.

Well, dearest, I had no notion what I was going to write, when I began; and indeed I doubted whether I should write anything at all; for after such intimate communion as that of our last blissful evening, it seems as if a sheet of paper could only be a veil betwixt us. Ownest, in the times that I have been speaking of, I used to think that I could imagine all passions, all feelings, all states of the heart and mind; but how little did I know what it is to be mingled with another's being! Thou only hast taught me that I have a heart—thou only hast thrown a light deep downward, and upward, into my soul. Thou only hast revealed me to myself; for without thy aid, my best knowledge of myself would have been merely to know my own shadow—to watch it flickering on the wall, and mistake its fantasies for my own real actions. Indeed, we are but shadows—we are not endowed with real life, and all that seems most real about us is but the thinnest substance of a dream—till the heart is touched. That touch creates us—then we begin to be—thereby we are beings of reality, and inheritors of eternity.

From a letter to G. S. Hillard
(16 July 1841)

I have not written that infernal story.[4] The thought of it has tormented me ever since I came here, and has deprived me of all the comfort I might otherwise have had, in my few moments of leisure. Thank God, it is now too late—so I disburthen my mind of it, now and forever.

You cannot think how exceedingly I regret the necessity of disappointing you; but what could be done? An engagement to write a story must in its nature be conditional; because stories grow like vegetables, and are not manufactured, like a pine table. My former stories all sprung up of their own accord, out of a quiet life. Now, I have no quiet at all; for when my outward man is at rest—which is seldom, and for short intervals—my mind is bothered with a sort of dull excitement, which makes it impossible to think continuously of any subject. You cannot make a silk purse out of a sow's ear; nor must you expect pretty stories from a man who feeds pigs.

My hands are covered with a new crop of blisters—the effect of raking hay; so excuse this scrawl.

Excerpt from a letter to G. S. Hillard, *The Centenary Edition*, 15:550. Copyright 1984 by Ohio State University Press. Reprinted with permission.

From a Letter to Sophia Peabody
(22 September 1841)

Belovedest, I doubt whether I shall succeed in writing another volume of Grandfather's Library,[5] while I remain at the farm. I have not the sense of perfect seclusion, which has always been essential to my power of producing anything. It is true, nobody intrudes into my room; but still I cannot be quiet. Nothing here is settled—everything is but beginning to arrange itself—and though thy husband would seem to have little to do with aught beside his own thoughts, still he cannot but partake of the ferment around him. My mind will not be abstracted. I must observe, and think, and feel, and content myself with catching glimpses of things which may be wrought out hereafter.

Excerpt from a letter to Sophia Peabody, *The Centenary Edition*, 15:575. Copyright 1984 by Ohio State University Press. Reprinted with permission.

From "The Custom-House" in
The Scarlet Letter

My imagination was a tarnished mirror. It would not reflect, or only with miserable dimness, the figures with which I did my best to people it. The characters of the narrative would not be warmed and rendered malleable, by any heat that I could kindle at my intellectual forge. They would take neither the glow of passion nor the tenderness of sentiment, but retained all the rigidity of dead corpses, and stared me in the face with a fixed and ghastly grin of contemptuous defiance. "What have you to do with us?" that expression seemed to say. "The little power you might once have possessed over the tribe of unrealities is gone! You have bartered it for a pittance of the public gold. Go, then, and earn your wages!" In short, the almost torpid creatures of my own fancy twitted me with imbecility, and not without fair occasion.

It was not merely during the three hours and a half which Uncle Sam claimed as his share of my daily life, that this wretched numbness held possession of me. It went with me on my sea-shore walks and rambles into the country, whenever—which was seldom and reluctantly—I bestirred myself to seek that invigorating charm of Nature, which used to give me such freshness and activity of thought, the moment that I stepped across the threshold of the Old Manse. The same torpor, as regarded the capacity for intellectual effort, accompanied me home, and weighed upon me in the chamber which I most absurdly termed my study. Nor did it quit me, when, late at night, I sat in the deserted parlour, lighted only by the glimmering coal-fire and the moon, striving to picture forth imaginary scenes, which, the next day, might flow out on the brightening page in many-hued description.

If the imaginative faculty refused to act at such an hour, it might well be deemed a hopeless case. Moonlight, in a familiar room, falling so white upon the carpet, and showing all its figures so distinctly,—making every object so minutely visible, yet so unlike a morning or noontide visibility,—is a medium the most suitable for a romance-writer to get acquainted with his illusive guests. There is the little domestic scenery of the well-known apartment; the chairs, with each its separate individuality; the centre-table, sustaining a workbasket, a volume or two, and an extinguished lamp; the sofa; the book-case; the picture on the wall;—all these details, so completely seen, are so spiritualized by the unusual light, that they seem to lose their actual substance, and become things of intellect. Nothing is too small or too trifling to undergo this change, and acquire dignity thereby. A child's shoe; the doll, seated in her little wicker carriage; the hobby-horse;—whatever, in a word, has been used or played with, during the day, is now invested with a quality of strangeness and remoteness, though still almost as vividly present as by daylight. Thus, therefore, the floor of our familiar room has become a neutral territory, somewhere between the real world and fairy-land, where the Actual and the Imaginary may meet, and each imbue itself with the nature of the other. Ghosts might enter here, without affrighting us. It would be too much in keeping with the scene to excite surprise, were we to look about us and discover a form, beloved, but gone hence, now sitting quietly in a streak of this magic moonshine, with an aspect that would make us doubt whether it had returned from afar, or had never once stirred from our fireside.

The somewhat dim coal-fire has an essential influence in producing the effect which I would describe. It throws its unobtrusive tinge throughout the room, with a faint ruddiness upon the walls and ceiling, and a reflected gleam from the polish of the furniture. This warmer light mingles itself with the cold spirituality of the moonbeams, and communicates, as it were, a heart and sensibilities of human tenderness to the forms which fancy summons up. It converts them from snow-images into men and women. Glancing at the looking-glass, we behold—deep within its haunted verge— the smouldering glow of the half-extinguished anthracite, the white moonbeams on the floor, and a repetition of all the gleam and shadow of the picture, with one remove farther from the actual, and nearer to the imaginative. Then, at such an hour, and with this scene before him, if a man, sitting all alone, cannot dream strange things, and make them look like truth, he need never try to write romances.

But, for myself, during the whole of my Custom-House experience, moonlight and sunshine, and the glow of firelight, were just alike in my regard; and neither of them was of one whit more avail than the twinkle of a tallow-candle. An entire class of susceptibilities, and a gift connected with them,—of no great richness or value, but the best I had,—was gone from me.

From a Letter to James T. Fields
(13 April 1854)

I am very glad that the "Mosses" have come into the hands of our firm; and I return the copy sent me, after a careful revision.[6] When I wrote those dreamy sketches, I little thought that I should ever prepare an edition for the press amidst the bustling life of a Liverpool consul. Upon my honor, I am not quite sure that I entirely comprehend my own meaning in some of these blasted allegories; but I remember that I always had a meaning—or, at least, thought I had. I am a good deal changed since those times; and to tell you the truth, my past self is not very much to my taste, as I see myself in this book. Yet certainly there is more in it than the public generally gave me credit for, at the time it was written. But I don't think myself worthy of very much more credit than I got. It has been a very disagreeable task to read the book.

Excerpt from a letter to James Fields, *The Centenary Edition*, 17:201. Copyright 1987 by Ohio State University Press. Reprinted with permission.

From *Our Old Home*

I once hoped, indeed, that so slight a volume would not be all that I might write. These and other sketches, with which, in a somewhat rougher form than I have given them here, my Journal was copiously filled, were intended for the side-scenes, and back-grounds, and exterior adornment, of a work of fiction, of which the plan had imperfectly developed itself in my mind, and into which I ambitiously proposed to convey more of various modes of truth than I could have grasped by a direct effort. Of course, I should not mention this abortive project, only that it has been utterly thrown aside, and will never now be accomplished. The Present, the Immediate, the Actual, has proved too potent for me.

Excerpt from *Our Old Home, The Centenary Edition*, 5:3–4. Copyright 1970 by Ohio State University Press. Reprinted with permission.

From a Letter to James T. Fields
(17 January 1864)

I am not quite up to writing yet, but shall make an effort as soon as I see any hope of success. You ought to be thankful that (like most other broken-down authors) I do not pester you with decrepit pages, and insist upon your accepting them as full of the old spirit and vigor. That trouble, perhaps, still awaits you, after I shall have reached a further stage of decay.

Seriously, my mind has, for the present, lost its temper and its fine edge, and I have an instinct that I had better keep quiet. Perhaps I shall have a new spirit of vigor, if I wait quietly for it—perhaps not.

Excerpt from a letter to James Fields, *The Centenary Edition*, 18:634. Copyright 1987 by Ohio State University Press. Reprinted with permission.

Notes to Part 2

1. Duyckinck had written: "There is no particular richness in the style: in some respects it is plain, but it flows on pellucid as a mountain rivulet, and you feel in its refreshing purity that it is fed by springs beneath."

2. *The Writings of Nathaniel Hawthorne* (Boston: Houghton, Mifflin and Company, 1900) 17:202–203.

3. I Kings 19:11.

4. For the 1842 *Token* edited by Hillard, and scheduled to be printed in the Autumn of 1841. This is probably the "annual to be published in Boston, and which is to be a fair specimen of the arts of this country,' . . . edited (*sub rosa*) by Longfellow, Felton, Hillard and that set" of which J. R. Lowell wrote to G. B. Loring 18 February 1841. Lowell wrote that he had been asked to contribute: "Hawthorne and Emerson are writing for it, and Bryant and Halleck have promised to write." See Horace E. Scudder, *James Russell Lowell: A Biography* (Boston: Houghton, Mifflin, 1901), I, 93.

5. *Biographical Stories for Children*, to be published 12 April 1842, in Boston by Tappan and Dennet.

6. Fields had first asked G. P. Putnam in March 1851 to sell the rights to *Mosses from an Old Manse*, but did not obtain them until March 1854. A second, enlarged edition was to be published by Ticknor & Fields on 18 September.

Part 3

_____

THE CRITICS

From the beginning of Hawthorne's career, when Henry Wadsworth Longfellow reviewed the first edition of *Twice-Told Tales*, Hawthorne's stories have attracted outstanding critics. Other writers commenting on Hawthorne include Herman Melville, Edgar Allan Poe, Anthony Trollope, William Dean Howells, Henry James, D. H. Lawrence, Jorge Luis Borges, T. S. Eliot, and Robert Penn Warren. The density of Hawthorne's best tales has also drawn an unending procession of scholarly interpreters, most reading the stories in terms of a particular aspect such as myth, religion, psychoanalysis, aesthetics, or feminism. All these approaches work because not only does Hawthorne successfully entertain a variety of perspectives in his short fiction, but each story can sustain diverse viewpoints.

I include a sampling of different kinds of analyses to indicate the broad variety and high quality of responses to Hawthorne's work. I hope this selection encourages other readers to trust and develop their own reactions to Hawthorne's tales, for the more perspectives Hawthorne critics acknowledge, the more they realize the values suggested by Hawthorne's short fiction.

I began with excerpts from Melville, Poe, and James to indicate Hawthorne's impact on nineteenth-century American literature and to emphasize the connection Melville and James assert between Hawthorne's writing and his character. Later critics take a more objective approach to Hawthorne's tales. Richard Harter Fogle offers a compelling analysis of ambiguity, Nina Baym examines their treatment of women, Michael Colacurcio looks at the role of history, and Gloria Ehrlich offers a biographical analysis. Other critics have used each of these approaches to Hawthorne's work, but Fogle, Baym, Colacurcio, and Ehrlich provide particularly strong models. Hawthorne scholars have also produced fine mythic, psychoanalytic, sociological, and religious interpretations as well as source studies and aesthetic analyses. I include some of these in the selective bibliography concluding this section.

Hawthorne and His Mosses

Herman Melville

But it is the least part of genius that attracts admiration. Where Hawthorne is known, he seems to be deemed a pleasant writer, with a pleasant style,—a sequestered, harmless man, from whom any deep and weighty thing would hardly be anticipated:—a man who means no meanings. But there is no man, in whom humor and love, like mountain peaks, soar to such a rapt height, as to receive the irradiations of the upper skies;—there is no man in whom humor and love are developed in that high form called genius; no such man can exist without also possessing, as the indispensable complement of these, a great, deep intellect, which drops down into the universe like a plummet. Or, love and humor are only the eyes, through which such an intellect views this world. The great beauty in such a mind is but the product of its strength. What, to all readers, can be more charming than the piece entitled "Monsieur du Miroir"; and to a reader at all capable of fully fathoming it, what, at the same time, can possess more mystical depth of meaning?—Yes, there he sits, and looks at me,—this "shape of mystery", this "identical Monsieur du Miroir"; and to a reader at all capable of fully fathoming it, what, at the same time, can possess more mystical depth of meaning?—Yes, there he sits, and looks at me,—this "shape of mystery", this "identical Monsieur du Miroir".—"Methinks I should tremble now, were his wizard power of gliding through all impediments in search of me, to place him suddenly before my eyes".

How profound, nay appalling, is the moral evolved by the "Earth's Holocaust"; where—beginning with the hollow follies and affectations of the world,—all vanities and empty theories and forms, are, one after another, and by an admirably graduated, growing comprehensiveness, thrown into the allegorical fire, till, at length, nothing is left but the all-engendering heart of man; which remaining still unconsumed, the great conflagration is nought.

Excerpted from Herman Melville, *The Piazza Tales*, ed. Harrison Hayford, Alma A. MacDougall, G. Thomas Tanselle, et al. The Writings of Herman Melville, The Northwestern-Newberry Edition, Volume IX. Copyright 1987, Northwestern University Press and the Newberry Library, Evanston and Chicago. Reprinted by permission.

Of a piece with this, is the "Intelligence Office", a wondrous symbolizing of the secret workings in men's souls. There are other sketches, still more charged with ponderous import.

"The Christmas Banquet", and "The Bosom Serpent" would be fine subjects for a curious and elaborate analysis, touching the conjectural parts of the mind that produced them. For spite of all the Indian-summer sunlight on the hither side of Hawthorne's soul, the other side—like the dark half of the physical sphere—is shrouded in a blackness, ten times black. But this darkness but gives more effect to the ever-moving dawn, that forever advances through it, and circumnavigates his world. Whether Hawthorne has simply availed himself of this mystical blackness as a means to the wondrous effects he makes it to produce in his lights and shades; or whether there really lurks in him, perhaps unknown to himself, a touch of Puritanic gloom,—this, I cannot altogether tell. Certain it is, however, that this great power of blackness in him derives its force from its appeals to that Calvinistic sense of Innate Depravity and Original Sin, from whose visitations, in some shape or other, no deeply thinking mind is always and wholly free. For, in certain moods, no man can weigh this world, without throwing in something, somehow like Original Sin, to strike the uneven balance. At all events, perhaps no writer has ever wielded this terrific thought with greater terror than this same harmless Hawthorne. Still more: this black conceit pervades him, through and through. You may be witched by his sunlight,—transported by the bright glidings in the skies he builds over you;—but there is the blackness of darkness beyond; and even his bright glidings but fringe, and play upon the edges of thunder-clouds.—In one word, the world is mistaken in this Nathaniel Hawthorne. He himself must often have smiled at its absurd misconception of him. He is immeasurably deeper than the plummet of the mere critic. For it is not the brain that can test such a man; it is only the heart. You cannot come to know greatness by inspecting it; there is no glimpse to be caught of it, except by intuition; you need not ring it, you but touch it, and you find it is gold.

*   *   *

Gainsay it who will, as I now write, I am Posterity speaking by proxy—and after times will make it more than good, when I declare—that the American, who up to the present day, has evinced, in Literature, the largest brain with the largest heart, that man is Nathaniel Hawthorne. Moreover, that whatever Nathaniel Hawthorne may hereafter write, "The Mosses from an Old Manse" will be ultimately accounted his masterpiece.

Hawthorne's "Tales"

Edgar Allan Poe

I must hasten to conclude this paper with a summary of Mr. Hawthorne's merits and demerits.

He is peculiar and not original—unless in those detailed fancies and detached thoughts which his want of general originality will deprive of the appreciation due to them, in preventing them from ever reaching the public eye. He is infinitely too fond of allegory, and can never hope for popularity so long as he persists in it. This he will not do, for allegory is at war with the whole tone of his nature, which disports itself never so well as when escaping from the mysticism of his "Goodman Browns" and "White Old Maids" into the hearty, genial, but still Indian-summer sunshine of his "Wakefields" and "Little Annie's Rambles." Indeed, his spirit of "metaphor run-mad" is clearly imbibed from the phalanx and phalanstery atmosphere in which he has been so long struggling for breath. He has not half the material for the exclusiveness of authorship that he possesses for its universality. He has the purest style, the finest taste, the most available scholarship, the most delicate humor, the most touching pathos, the most radiant imagination, the most consummate ingenuity; and with these varied good qualities he has done *well* as a mystic. But is there any one of these qualities which should prevent his doing doubly as well in a career of honest, upright, sensible, prehensible, and comprehensible things? Let him mend his pen, get a bottle of visible ink, come out from the Old Manse, cut Mr. Alcott, hang (if possible) the editor of the "Dial," and throw out of the window to the pigs all his odd numbers of the "North American Review."

Excerpted from *The Works of Edgar Allan Poe*, ed. Edmund Stedman and George Woodberry (Chicago: Stone & Kimball, 1895), 7:37–38.

Hawthorne

Henry James

Certainly, as a general thing, we are struck with the ingenuity and felicity of Hawthorne's analogies and correspondences; the idea appears to have made itself at home in them easily. Nothing could be better in this respect than *The Snow Image* (a little masterpiece), or *The Great Carbuncle*, or *Doctor Heidegger's Experiment*, or *Rappacini's Daughter*. But in such things as *The Birth-Mark* and *The Bosom-Serpent* we are struck with something stiff and mechanical, slightly incongruous, as if the kernel had not assimilated its envelope. But these are matters of light impression, and there would be a want of tact in pretending to discriminate too closely among things which all, in one way or another, have a charm. The charm—the great charm—is that they are glimpses of a great field, of the whole deep mystery of man's soul and conscience. They are moral, and their interest is moral; they deal with something more than the mere accidents and conventionalities, the surface occurrences of life. The fine thing in Hawthorne is that he cared for the deeper psychology, and that, in his way, he tried to become familiar with it. This natural, yet fanciful, familiarity with it; this air, on the author's part, of being a confirmed *habitué* of a region of mysteries and subtleties, constitutes the originality of his tales. And then they have the further merit of seeming, for what they are, to spring up so freely and lightly. The author has all the case, indeed, of a regular dweller in the moral, psychological realm; he goes to and fro in it, as a man who knows his way. His tread is a light and modest one, but he keeps the key in his pocket.

His little historical stories all seem to me admirable; they are so good that you may re-read them many times. They are not numerous, and they are very short; but they are full of a vivid and delightful sense of the New England past; they have, moreover, the distinction, little tales of a dozen and fifteen pages as they are, of being the only successful attempts at historical fiction that have been made in the United States. Hawthorne was at home in the early New England history; he had thumbed its records and he had breathed its air, in whatever odd receptacles this

Excerpted from *Hawthorne* (New York: Harper & Brothers, 1879), 63–64.

somewhat pungent compound still lurked. He was fond of it, and he was proud of it, as any New Englander must be, measuring the part of that handful of half-starved fanatics who formed his earliest precursors, in laying the foundations of a mighty empire. Hungry for the picturesque as he always was, and not finding any very copious provision of it around him, he turned back into the two preceding centuries, with the earnest determination that the primitive annals of Massachusetts should at least *appear* picturesque. His fancy, which was always alive, played a little with the somewhat meagre and angular facts of the colonial period, and forthwith converted a great many of them into impressive legends and pictures. There is a little infusion of colour, a little vagueness about certain details, but it is very gracefully and discreetly done, and realities are kept in view sufficiently to make us feel that if we are reading romance, it is romance that rather supplements than contradicts history.

Hawthorne's Fiction:
The Light and the Dark
Richard Harter Fogle

The essence of Hawthorne is, in fact, distilled from the opposing elements of simplicity and complexity. This essence is a clear liquid, with no apparent cloudiness. Hawthorne, together with Henry James, perhaps, is the only American novelist who has been able to see life whole without, in Thackeray's words, "roaring ai, ai, as loud as Prometheus," like Melville, Wolfe, and Faulkner; droning interminably an account of its details, like Dreiser; or falling into a thin, shrill irony, the batlike twittering of souls in Hades, like all the sad young men. Hawthorne's tone is equable, "not harsh nor grating, but with ample power to chasten and subdue." He is a unique and wonderful combination of light and darkness.

The light in Hawthorne is clarity of design. He has a classic balance; his language is exquisitely lucid. He gives one the sense of an invulnerable dignity and centrality; he is impenetrably self-possessed. He holds his characters to the highest standards, for he literally brings them to judgment at the bar of eternity as immortal souls. The "dark" in Hawthorne, that blackness which Herman Melville applauded in him, is his tragic complexity. His clarity is intermingled with subtlety, his statement interfused with symbolism, his affirmation enriched with ambiguity. The whole which results is captivating. In attack he is mild but deadly. His blow is so delicately delivered that a man would have to turn his head in order to realize that he had just lost it. "The Custom House" essay, for example, which rather oddly precedes *The Scarlet Letter*, seems at first sight merely agreeable. Look closer, however, and the effect is devastating. These gently humorous character portraits are murderous, not from malice or heat, but from judgment and icy cold. Hawthorne is not indignant; he is merely certain of his grounds. And his certainty is that of one whose father was called "the sternest man who ever walked a deck."

Excerpted from *Hawthorne's Fiction: The Light & the Dark*, by Richard Harter Fogle, 4–7. Copyright © 1952 by the University of Oklahoma Press.

He is so entirely unsentimental that he does not need, as we sometimes do, to avoid sentimentality. He combines sympathy with a classic aloofness, participation with cool observation. "My father," said Julian Hawthorne, "was two men, one sympathetic and intuitional, the other critical and logical; together they formed a combination which could not be thrown off its feet." Thus Hawthorne's writing has a tone of exquisite gravity, harmonized strangely with a pervasive irony and humor. In the use of irony he is a lighter, more sensitive Fielding, with depths besides which Fielding could not plumb. In the matter of irony Hawthorne's antecedents in the eighteenth-century novel might well be re-examined.

Corresponding to the clarity and the complexity of Hawthorne are his "philosophy" and the crosscurrents which modify its course. For the best understanding one should always attend to the thought of the author. But one grasps that author wholly only by observing his characters, his settings, the patterns of his diction, the trends of his imagery, the concrete mechanics of telling a story. What one has grasped is admittedly not easy to describe, however—therefore the advantage of seizing upon the writer's thought, which can be systematically abstracted.

The philosophy of Hawthorne is a broadly Christian scheme which contains heaven, earth, and hell. Whether heaven and hell are realities or only subjective states of mind is one of Hawthorne's crucial ambiguities. I do not call him a Christian humanist, as do some excellent critics, for it seems to me that heaven and hell *are* real to him and play too large a part in his fiction to be relegated to the background. In his mixed macrocosm, man is a microcosm also mixed. Man's chief temptation is to forget his limits and complexities, to think himself all good, or to think himself all bad. Either way he falls into spiritual isolation and pride. He needs a proper mixture of the earthly and the ideal—with a touch of the flame to temper it. Thus Aylmer, the scientist-hero of "The Birthmark," violates the covenant of humankind when he tries to eradicate the only blemish of his beautiful wife, a tiny mark on her cheek. He succeeds, but kills her in the process. The birthmark, which is shaped like a hand, is her grip upon earthly existence. She dies to the sound of the laughter of Aminadab, Aylmer's assistant, a kind of earthfiend. Even the pit has its claims, which must not be slighted. The conclusion epitomizes Hawthorne's thinking: ". . . had Aylmer reached a profounder wisdom, he need not thus have flung away the happiness which would have woven his mortal life of the selfsame texture with the celestial. The momentary circumstance was too strong for him; he failed to look beyond the shadowy scope of time, and living once for all in eternity, to find the perfect future in the present." There is a time for everything, and an eternity. Aylmer should have waited.

But the system does not make the story. The tale of "The Minister's Black Veil" will illustrate the difference between an abstract and a literary meaning. The minister dons the veil as an emblem of secret sin, of which all men are presumably guilty. Elizabeth, his betrothed, implores him to discard it. The minister has found a dreadful truth, while Elizabeth may have discovered a greater—that men are evil *and also* good. The meaning lies not in either but in both. So Hawthorne condemns his strange seekers, his Aylmers, his Ethan Brands, but he makes them noble. His reconciliation is not finally in logic, for he accepts the mystery of existence. His reconciliation is the acceptance itself, realized in balance, structure, and tone.

Thwarted Nature: Hawthorne as Feminist

Nina Baym

A list of the short stories in which the theme of woman structures the action is, in the main, a list of those short works on which Hawthorne criticism of the last few decades has concentrated. In chronological order these are "Roger Malvin's Burial" (1832), "Wakefield" (1835), "Young Goodman Brown" (1835), "The Minister's Black Veil" (1836), "The Prophetic Pictures" (1837), "The Shaker Bridal" (1838), "Sylph Etherege" (1838), "The Birthmark" (1843), "Egotism, or, the Bosom Serpent" (1843), "Rappaccini's Daughter" (1844), "The Artist of the Beautiful" (1844), "Drowne's Wooden Image" (1844), and "Ethan Brand" (1849). (I omit from this list stories in which women characters have no special gender reference, such as "The Great Carbuncle" or "Dr. Heidegger's Experiment," and stories in which the theme is present but not controlling, as in the minor sexual sadism of "Endicott and the Red Cross," "The Snow Image," and "The Hollow of the Three Hills," or the prurient relation between narrator and female auditors in "Alice Doane's Appeal." Among stories included, only "Sylph Etherege" can be considered minor, and only a few major stories—"My Kinsman, Major Molyneux" (1832), "The May-Pole of Merry Mount" (1836), and "The Legends of the Province-House" (1838 and 1839)— are absent.)

In general terms which, admittedly, require qualification or sophistication in specific instances, these stories narrate the rejection, by a man, of a sexual union with a woman who is either his fiancée or his wife. This rejection affects both man and woman adversely and, in the woman's case, often fatally. Reuben Bourne's slaying of his son may not kill Dorcas, his wife, in "Roger Malvin's Burial" for Hawthorne writes only "She heard him not. With one wild shriek, that seemed to force its way from the sufferer's inmost soul, she sank insensible by the side of her dead boy." But there is no question about the death of Martha in "The

Excerpted from "Thwarted Nature: Nathaniel Hawthorne as Feminist" by Nina Baym. Reprinted with permission of G. K. Hall, an imprint of Macmillan Publishing Company, from AMERICAN NOVELISTS REVISITED: Essays in Feminist Criticism, edited by Fritz Fleischmann. Copyright © 1982 by Fritz Fleischmann.

Shaker Bridal," or about its cause: "But paler and paler grew Martha by his side, till, like a corpse in its burial clothes, she sank down at the feet of her early lover; for, after many trials firmly borne, her heart could endure the weight of its desolate agony no longer" (9:425); nor about the death of Georgiana in "The Birthmark": "The birthmark—the sole token of human imperfection—faded from her cheek, the parting breath of the now perfect woman passed into the atmosphere, and her soul, lingering a moment near her husband, took its heavenward flight" (10:56); nor about that of Beatrice, killed by two men: "and thus the poor victim of man's ingenuity and of thwarted nature, and of the fatality that attends all such efforts of perverted wisdom, perished there, at the feet of her father and Giovanni" (10:128). The recurrent image of a woman dead at a man's feet and through his efforts cannot be ignored.

What exactly are the efforts that lead to this grim result? In most of the stories written before the Old Manse period, that is, before 1842, the destruction or damaging of the woman seems to result accidentally as a by-product, so to speak, of other intentions. Critics argue endlessly about whether Reuben Bourne meant to kill his son Cyrus, but nobody doubts that the damage to Dorcas was unintentional. As a result of putting on the black veil, either to make a statement to his parishioners or to hide a real secret, Reverend Hooper dooms his fiancée Elizabeth to lifelong spinsterhood; but it does not seem that he devised his plan in order thus to ruin her life. Wakefield, apparently, left home on a whim and not out of malice toward the woman he thereby "widowed"; and he returns after twenty years in the same spirit, not purposefully to bring about, once again, a total disruption of her peaceful life. Young Goodman Brown casts off Faith as a result of his forest experience, but it hardly seems likely that he entered the forest in order to find a pretext for denying her. On the contrary: "Well; she's a blessed angel on earth; and after this one night, I'll cling to her skirts and follow her to Heaven" (10:75).

But does the protagonist not protest too much? The question of a covert intention cannot be entirely absent. If these men did not devise patterns of behavior calculated to destroy the women who love them, they certainly failed signally to think of the possible effect that their plans might have on these women. At the very least—and to this, Hawthorne certainly commits his narrative voice—these are selfish men, basically indifferent to women. That indifference seems to be the source of their killing power so far as women are concerned; its result is the "thwarted nature" described in "Rappaccini's Daughter." Certainly, a supreme selfishness motivates Adam Colburn when he suggests to Martha Pierson, who has waited half a lifetime to marry him, that they join the Shakers. To Adam no sacrifice is involved in sacrificing sexual union; but this is not true for Martha, for whom, with her "woman's heart, and a tender one," there is "something awful and horrible in her situation and destiny" (9:424, 423).

The women in these stories have very slight presences, but these presences are always intensely physical and domestic. In the physical attachment to a man they are fulfilled and offer fulfillment. Thus, Dorcas lives contentedly with her gloomy husband Reuben Bourne and is not sad to leave society with him, "for she felt that it was better to journey in the wilderness, with two whom she loved, than to be a lonely woman in a crowd that cared not for her" (10:357). The physicality of the tie is suggested not only by Martha's agony in a sexless union, but by the "tie" of Faith's pink ribbons and numerous other concrete symbols that link the saving power of the woman with her body and through her body to Nature.

Perhaps the trite critical discussions of head versus heart in Hawthorne's writing will come to mind here—women as heart, men as head. Yet if the "heart" stands for body, and the "head" for rejection of the body, then it seems more accurate to identify the opposition as sexual passion versus the lack of it. The loving heart of woman is closely identified with, even an iconographic substitute for, a warm sexuality, whereas the stone man, "The Man of Adamant," the man in whom head predominates, is sexually frozen. The evidence of his coldness, however the evidence is made manifest in action, is what truly kills the woman. To reject her sexually is to reject her fatally. She dies. The man goes on living, but he is merely a shell.

Let us remember here that these stories are making statements not about the real nature of women but about the way in which men imagine them. As is so common in the Judeo-Christian tradition, the woman has become the locus of physicality; what is unusual in these writings is the degree to which the protagonist does not seem to recognize any "temptation" in these women. The body simply does not interest him and the woman who is "in" her body and identified with that body suffers from neglect rather than cruelty. However, the stories associated with the Old Manse era in Hawthorne's life escalate the man's indifference to an attitude more clearly hostile. And, where women in the earlier group of stories were, apparently, inadvertently caught up and victimized by the man's obsession, woman herself is now the obsession. Retroactively, these two stories force us to inquire if perhaps women were not always, in some disguised sense, the Hawthorne male's obsession.

Specifically, some aspect of the woman is the obsession: some aspect of her body. The hero attempts to purify the woman by separating her in some way from her body. This, as Hawthorne recognizes, is murder: sex-murder. For Aylmer in "The Birthmark," the hand-shaped mark on his wife's cheek becomes the locus of his demonic energies; for Giovanni in "Rappaccini's Daughter," it is the entire physical presence of Beatrice, her very body itself especially as concentrated in her fragrance, her physical perfume, that revolts him. In both these instances, it is impossible to distinguish revulsion from attraction, for exactly to the extent that these men are obsessed, possessed, with the woman's body they are revolted by it. I think we must say that these men actually perceive attraction as what we would think of as its opposite—repulsion. That is to say, they experience a physical sensation which they interpret as repulsion where, to us, it looks exactly like attraction. The intellectual trickery by which one sensation is transformed into or interpreted as its opposite occurs at a level beneath the awareness of the self-confident protagonist, but not so far beneath awareness as to preclude the faint suggestion that some degree of self-delusion may be involved. And, regardless of the need to speak a guarded language, imposed by the mores of his day and the extreme sensitivity of his subject, the narrator is not deceived.

Hawthorne has engaged here with the moral code that makes sex an unnatural act. Or, more precisely, he is engaged with that part of the psyche—of the male psyche—that perceives sex as an unnatural act and therefore produces such moral codes. But by linking the woman's saving grace and her body inseparably, Hawthorne is indicating that if anything is unnatural, it is the part of the psyche that repudiates human sexuality. He shows us men who, shocked and horrified by the human female body, are driven to dissociate themselves from the entire social fabric as a means of protecting themselves from it. He shows us men for whom evidence of women's sexual responsiveness is sufficient to cause an existential breakdown: "My Faith is gone! . . . There is no good on earth; and sin is but a name. Come, devil! for to thee is this world given" (10:83). But this is not all. He also shows men who, while rejecting real women who unavoidably inhabit physical bodies, substitute fantasies of them that are truly unnatural, fantasies of lust, power, degradation, and control. These fantasies are the outgrowth of the unnatural male psyche.

Certainly we engage here with that familiar modern lament about the growth of mind and self-consciousness in the human being as a result of which he is irrevocably sundered from nature. And in the debate over whether mind is man's glory or his curse, Hawthorne would seem to be taking the "romantic" view that it is his curse. "Woman" would appear to be playing the familiar part of the "Other" in this scheme, and as women suffer in Hawthorne's stories, real women suffer from a peculiar double bind: though made to suffer as bodies, they are denied existence as mind. But Hawthorne is not simply using women to signify nature and the other, and he is not really concerned with abstract romantic self-consciousness. He is suggesting, rather, that the male inability to deal with woman's body is the *source* of all the abstract formulations that function as so many defenses against, and diversions from, the truth. Behind Goodman Brown's religious rhetoric, behind Aylmer's scientific pose, behind Owen Warland's artistic vocation, behind Giovanni's moral crusade, lurk the manifold emotions that prevent men from making connection with women. These emotions, unknowable and unnameable, reach the light of day, as it were, in fantasy. And fantasy is what obsesses Hawthorne as an artist.

This obsession—Hawthorne's obsession—is felt in passage after passage. Consider the initiation scene in "Young Goodman Brown" as an example. In the depths of the forest, the devil delivers his sermon to the novitiates, among whom are Brown and Faith. He catalogs a sequence of "secret deeds" each more awful than the one before. And, "yet, far more than this!" he promises them, "It shall be yours to penetrate, in every bosom, the deep mystery of sin, the fountain of all wicked arts, and which inexhaustibly supplies more evil impulses than human power—than my power, at its utmost!—can make manifest in deed" (10:87). The impulses that produce real crimes originate in fantasy, which is infinitely energetic, infinitely productive. Fantasy becomes as evil as action, perhaps more so.

"The husband cast one look at his pale wife, and Faith at him. What polluted wretches would the next glance shew them to each other, shuddering alike at what they disclosed and what they saw!" (10:88). Although neither Goodman Brown nor Faith has been given a background or a history in any detail, Hawthorne has told us enough about these two so that we can assert with confidence that neither has ever performed any of the evil deeds catalogued by the devil. But they have fantasized—as the devil says, everybody has. The only pollution that the text can imply, at this point in the tale, is the secret pollution of the human bosom, the secret of its fantasies.

Now, if Young Goodman Brown did not "actually" attend a witch's meeting but only dreamed that he did, then that dream—which so prominently features the depiction of his wife as polluted—is itself such an evil fantasy, so the infinite world of fantasy is not escaped by calling Brown's adventure a dream. And so, too, is "Young Goodman Brown" an evil fantasy, featuring so prominently its vision of secret evil and implying so many more awful imaginings than it articulates.

Now Hawthorne did not give all his creative energies in his "early phase"—the years preceding his employment in the Salem customhouse—to the kind of story we have been examining. He alternated between these and light sketches, plotless short pieces which developed a sequence of images and incidents organized sometimes as a procession or a panorama but frequently developed simply as exercises in free association. Modern criticism, however, has characterized most of these sketches as secondary achievements, weak performances, because of their general insubstantiality, triteness, and a prettiness of both matter and rhetoric. Hawthorne's narrator seems to agree, using such images of evanescence for this type of work as snowflakes, dewdrops, or footprints on the sandy shore.

The material that we find at once more powerful and more typical of Hawthorne's imagination consists of the stories of harm. These stories are divorced from the narrator by means of the narrative which he pretends to be purveying rather than creating, and on which he comments, often disapprovingly. Thus, those of Hawthorne's works that we consider to be his best generally include an authorial disclaimer, a suggestion either that Hawthorne was uncomfortable with the material or that he anticipated discomfort or disapproval in his audience. Yet, these "disclaimed" or heavily mediated stories represent, to us, the author's strong achievements! Our own critical judgment appears to support Hawthorne's sense that there is a close but unhealthy relationship between artistic and sexual power. Art is an expression of deformed sexuality, for its obsessive fantasy is that of doing harm to a woman. Sometimes Hawthorne represents this deformity as his own oddity, sometimes as his culture's curse, and sometimes as the nature of men.

The Province of Piety: Moral History in Hawthorne's Early Tales
An Excerpt Concerning "Roger Malvin's Burial"

Michael J. Colacurcio

Most obviously, Hawthorne's introductory remarks intend to remind us that "Lovewell's Fight" has not been in *every* way "well-remembered." The quotation marks around the event in question call our attention to the fact that it already has a literary status: as in most such cases, a chance skirmish has had to acquire a definite denomination, even as it was retrospectively judged to possess some definitive significance. And in this instance, even the level of diction suggested by "Fight" gives the case away. We know that literature has operated, and we suspect that myth may be involved as well, even before we advert to the dismal facts of the historical situation. Once we remember these facts, we instantly know how to proceed.

Having set out on an officially sponsored (if personally motivated) scalphunting expedition, Captain Lovewell's irregular troops began by slaughtering a party of Indians in their sleep. So much for vengeance. In the aftermath of this lucky (and profitable—for they were to receive a bounty of 100 pounds for each scalp) raid, they went on to bungle their own mercenary strategy by the tactic of pursuing a lone Indian in such a manner as to get themselves ambushed; and in the bloody "Fight" that followed they were to suffer great (and needless) losses from among their own number. Worst of all, according to the excessively nice morality of the time and place, they had engaged in this ill-advised piece of heroism on the Sabbath, when Divine Service recommended itself as a more fitting occupation than Search and Destroy. Possibly some of the men who survived (either the battle or the temptation to desert), and who managed to straggle back to civilization, actually had some sense that their enterprise would not bear much looking into; nevertheless, some of them seem to have told the truth. Other, more decorous observers saw at once the obvious advantages of turning the affair into a ballad. At least one such "historian" seems to have had the quite local motives of small-town friendship and family ties. But presumably anybody might perceive, in this instance at least, the superiority of some chivalric myth over the altogether unlovely facts of the case.[1]

And so a "story" about daring, loyalty, and personal heroism came into existence (and print) almost at once. Lovewell's men ceased to be bounty hunters and became selfless patriots and courageous heroes. Furthermore—in a small move that has the most astonishing significance for the interpretation of "Roger Malvin's Burial"—the date of the bloody "Fight" was moved back from Sunday (May 9) to Saturday (May 8). Many people knew better, but apparently no one protested; thus the matter passed into the folklore of the region. And thus the "story" was still being re-told as the "event" was ceremoniously memorialized in 1825. Small wonder, perhaps, if the same writer who (half-seriously) proposed building a monument on Gallows Hill (to balance the one at Bunker's) should have his own word to say about the one gradually taking substance at "Lovewell's Pond."[2]

Accordingly, "imagination" would indeed have to cast "certain circumstances judicially into the shade" before seeing "much to admire in the heroism of a little band who gave battle to twice their number in the heart of the enemy's country" (337); what seems a conventional enough justification of the tedious claim of "romance" to some "neutral territory" is actually a rather fierce (if obvious) attack on the most debased form of literary lying. If "chivalry itself might not blush to record the deeds of one or two individuals," the reason is only partly that one or two individuals probably did act bravely in a basically depraved situation; the other and more telling reason is that "chivalry itself"—as it was taught in the textbooks of the day, and as it went on from there to influence the standards of heroism operative in the pages of contemporary romance—seemed to possess a fairly high threshold of shame and could be made to countenance similar acts of moral desperation.[3] And finally, as we slide from the airy realm of heroic ideals into the real world of might-politics, everybody can at least confess some minimum pragmatic justification of the "end" of "Lovewell's Fight," whatever the mean-ness of its motives: "The battle, though so fatal to those who fought, was *not unfortunate* [my italics] in its consequences to the country; for it broke the strength of a tribe and conduced to the peace which subsisted during *several* [again, mine] years" (337). The irony reeks: the ballads we read, from then and now, ask us to renew our national purpose at the shrine of an event which purchased a few years of freedom for imperialistic expansion at the price of a carnage originally inspired by intentions equally materialistic and altogether less grand.[4] Perhaps we should examine our national conscience—or, if our own intentions are pure, re-examine the facts on which we hope to base a national literature.

The burden of Hawthorne's historical intention becomes clear as soon as we realize the extent to which Reuben Bourne functions as an "historian": he has, after all, lived through an event in which the whole community is interested; and he is their only available source of vital information. Thus we need to re-examine the dynamics of his own manifest failure to tell the whole truth in the context of the relation between the historian and the community whose image and identity he necessarily serves. And even his own drastically personal self-destruction may enact—or predict—some dire public consequence which may be expected to follow from a lie about origins.[5]

Reuben's own deep division of motive, based on a fundamental conflict of values, may or may not reflect the sort of self-division experienced by any of the actual survivors of the Lovewell farce; but his manipulation of the truth, in accordance with the conventionally heroic expectations of his "audience," perfectly recapitulates the process by which a trivial and ugly (if also, in some sense, a necessary) event had been transformed into an heroic story. We have seen how, by one account, Reuben lies to Dorcas *exactly as* he had lied to himself. We have also noticed how the "second" event seems to infect the "first," rendering the two not-different from a moral point of view. We are now in a position to see the full implication of this fact. Reuben lies to himself because of Dorcas and the community whose standards she embodies. He lies to himself precisely *because* he knows he will be unable to face her, and them, with a faithful narrative of the grisly realities of Love and Death in the American Wilderness: it was Malvin alone or Malvin and me too—just as it had been, at the outset, them (the Indians) or us (the White Provincials). The situation is inherently objectionable; no concept and no language can redeem it, though the utilitarian realism of Malvin seems closer to the mark than the sentimental idealism of Dorcas. Malvin is dying, however, and it is to Dorcas that Reuben must report. And in this case, unfortunately, the expectation of the audience infects the veracity of the reporter. He tells her exactly what he knows she wants to believe: that everybody in question acted with story-book bravery and that (therefore) things came out cleanly and for the best, if not quite happily.

Notes

1. Eckstorm's principal villain is Parson Symmes; but she also makes it clear that "everybody in official circles must have known," and that "no one hindered him" in his instant revision of history [Fanny Hardy Eckstorm, "Pigwacket and Parson Symmes," *New England Quarterly* 9 (1936): 401–402].

2. The *physical* monument to Lovewell was constructed only in 1904, but Bickford indicates that "it had always been the custom to conduct visitors . . . to the battleground at Lovewell's Pond" [Gail H. Bickford, "Lovewell's Fight, 1725–1958," *American Quarterly* 10 (1958): 363–4].

3. Robert Daly, "History and Chivalric Myth in 'Roger Malvin's Burial,'" *Essex Institute Historical Collections* 109 (1978): 112.

4. Ely Stock, "History and Bible in 'Roger Malvin's Burial,'" *Essex Institute Historical Collections* 100 (1964): 280–2.

5. The brief suggestion of Diane C. Naples is essentially apt: "'Roger Malvin's Burial' . . . may be Hawthorne's parable for the nineteenth-century historian"; see "'Roger Malvin's Burial—A Parable for Historians?" *American Transcendental Quarterly* 13 (1972): 45–48.

Family Themes and Hawthorne's Fiction: The Tenacious Web

Gloria Ehrlich

In "The Artist of the Beautiful" the conflict moves from that of mindlessly benevolent father against artistic children to the displaced family triangle that we have so often noted in Hawthorne's work. Here the prudent, skeptical materialism of Annie Hovenden's father diminishes the self-respect of his undersized, unworldly apprentice, thus intensifying the dynamics of Hawthorne's characteristic male relationship. To the detriment of his story, he so polarizes the antithesis that Owen Warland becomes a ludicrous child-man and Peter Hovenden a devil of malevolent skepticism, each intensifying the extremism of the other.

In couching such an unrelenting allegory of matter and spirit in the terms of his father-surrogate relationship, Hawthorne risks much artistically, but his purpose may have been more therapeutic than artistic. At the time of writing, in 1844, he was facing the impracticality of his literary vocation as the economic support for his growing family. In this year of Una's birth he was living cheaply at the Old Manse but earning little and, though dedicating himself to writing, not producing much in quantity or quality. His lack of literary success and the realities of his family situation may have reawakened the disapproving voice of his guardian chiding him for not taking up more manly and remunerative work. Although happy in his family situation he may even have felt the absence of a familiar goad since the death of Uncle Robert two years earlier. Lacking any overt opposition from Uncle Robert and languishing instead in Sophia's enthusiastic encouragement, he may have written this strange story in order to reawaken the counterforce that had previously helped define him as an artist and piqued him into productivity. In this story he marshalls his arguments against the internalized avuncular figure in order to rouse himself into renewed creative activity.

Paradoxically, Peter Hovenden's materialistic influence helps to shape Owen Warland's artistic career by repeatedly challenging his creative spirit: "There was nothing so antipodal to his nature as this man's cold, unimaginative sagacity, by contact with which everything was converted into a dream, except the densest matter of the physical world. Owen . . . prayed fervently to be delivered from him. . . . Owen never met this man without a shrinking of the heart. Of all the world, he was the most terrible, by reason of a keen understanding, which saw so distinctly what it did see, and disbelieved so uncompromisingly in what it could not see" (X, 456 and 463). Hovenden's unimaginative utilitarianism and Robert Danforth's virile strength diminish Owen's personal life but by their very opposition serve to refine, or to Platonize, his conception of art. Peter Hovenden is Annie's father and Robert Danforth becomes her husband. Annie serves as Owen's muse, but her father is more important in shaping his career.

Hawthorne was trying to work out serious personal and vocational problems in this story. His reduction of Owen's physical self to elfin dimensions is a bizarre way of expressing the insubstantiality he felt vis-à-vis men of action. Against little Owen are two such men, a skeptical older one who denigrates the impracticality of his endeavors and a brawny younger one who is Hovenden's ideal of young manhood—a blacksmith, a worker in iron, a laborer among realities, and therefore worthy of wife and family. Each intrusion of the Hovendens into Owen's private world causes a destruction of his work following which Owen declines morally and physically, first into drunkenness, then into infantile obesity, and finally into spiritual lethargy. When not functioning artistically, the story implies, the artist is even grosser, more material, than the reality-oriented men he scorns. If he cannot be more than such men, he becomes less. Owen regresses into a deep sloth that eventually proves to be not a death but a sleep of the spirit, a prerequisite to his spiritualization of matter, his one great burst of achievement. Owen's butterfly, like Hawthorne's story, is an allegory of self- and artistic reintegration. Like a real butterfly, Owen emerges from a wormlike condition after a period of dormancy to enjoy a brief moment of flight that justifies all the preparation. In putting Owen through phases of creativity and decline, periods of energetic invention, then successive destructions of his work followed by intervals of lethargy, Hawthorne was examining his own oscillations. Combating doubts about himself and his work, he used the story to revive the drama of psychic antitheses that had so long stimulated his artistic energies.

Owen works to spiritualize the clockwork mechanism, a measure of time that in youth he scorned in favor of eternal values. But the artist trying to transcend time is yet in his own person subject to time as measured out by his inner clock and the rhythms of his creative ebb and flow. The forty-year-old author who had not yet validated his artistic vocation with a substantial book was surely invested in the long disquisition on time, death, and the artist that follows immediately on Owen's recovery of his talents: "He was incited to toil the more diligently, by an anxiety lest death should surprise him in the midst of his labors. This anxiety, perhaps, is common to all men who set their hearts upon anything so high. . . . that life becomes of importance only as conditional to its accomplishment. So long as we love life for itself, we seldom dread losing it. When we desire life for the attainment of an object, we recognize the frailty of its texture" (X, 466–467). Owen Warland, the superior watchmaker, tries to transcend time much as his creator tried to idealize the actualities of daily life, but neither could do so without first incorporating the message of time. Spurred by chronological urgencies to deeper integration of this message, both had first to conquer the time-consuming sin of spiritual sloth, which today is more often called depression.

More pointedly, both transcended their own deficiencies by incorporating and inwardly transforming their materialistic opposites. In his deepest stage of regression and just before his final reawakening, Owen had lost his "faith in the invisible" and come to trust only "what his hand could touch" (X, 466), and in these terms he presents his mechanical marvel to Annie, now Mrs. Robert Danforth, "You shall know, and see, and touch, and possess, the secret" (X, 469). Before presenting his life's work to Annie and her "iron men" Owen has come to terms with their incomprehension and prepared himself for the philistine reception that his work indeed receives: "He knew that the world, *and Annie as the representative of the world*, whatever praise might be bestowed, could never say the fitting word, nor feel the fitting sentiment which should be the perfect recompense of an artist. . . . Not at this latest moment, was he to learn that the reward of all high performance must be sought within itself or sought in vain" (X, 472–473; italics added). But even in this exalted state Owen is not above feeling a "secret scorn" for the incomprehension behind Annie's wondering admiration, a scorn so subtle that only an artist would discern it. Annie's role as uncomprehending muse (itself a product of the artist's enhancing imagination) is a lesser stimulus to the creative process than is her father's belittling provocation. Like the author putting his book before the public, Owen has prepared himself in advance for the world's response and, in anticipation, largely risen above it. Having recognized the Doubting Thomas within himself, he can forgive it in others. Realizing that in the process of producing the work he has become a different person from the one who conceived it, he discovers that the butterfly now has a different meaning for him. He can do without the perceptible representation of his ideal, for his real achievement is in what he has become, and this his public and perhaps even his muse, cannot fully appreciate. In this odd little story we can see the forty-year-old Hawthorne reviving his old antagonist in order to rally himself for a renewed assault on the citadel of fame and rehearsing various prospective scripts for the outcome. Should he fail to achieve fame he could always dismiss it as "the last infirmity of noble minds."

Chronology

4 July 1804–Nathaniel Hawthorne is born in Salem, Massachusetts, the son of Nathaniel Hawthorne, a sailor, and Elizabeth Clarke Manning. His older sister, Elizabeth Manning, was born 7 March 1802. A younger sister, Maria Louisa, is born 9 January 1808. His father dies while at sea in April 1808. In July 1808, Hawthorne's mother moves her family into her parents' household in Salem. Her eight unmarried brothers and sisters lavish attention on her children.

10 November 1813—Hawthorne is injured while playing ball. The resulting lameness keeps him from attending regular school until February 1816.

June 1916—Hawthorne's immediate family goes to Raymond, Maine, where they intend to settle with his uncle Robert Manning. The young Nathaniel enjoys living in the country and reluctantly returns to school in Salem in October. The rest of the family follows in the spring. In October 1818, Nathaniel's family moves to Raymond, but on 16 December, Nathaniel is taken to a boarding school run by the Reverend Caleb Bradley in Stroudwater, Maine.

June 1819—Hawthorne is sent to Salem to live in the Manning house and attend Samuel H. Archer's school. In March 1820, he begins college preparatory studies with Benjamin Lynde Oliver.

28 September 1821—Hawthorne enters Bowdoin college in Brunswick, Maine, the first member of his family to attend college. Here he becomes close friends with Horatio Bridge, Franklin Pierce, Jonathan Cilley, and an acquaintance of Henry Wadsworth Longfellow. Hawthorne graduates on 7 September 1825, eighteenth a class of thirty-eight.

September 1825—Hawthorne returns to his mother's household in Salem where he begins to write. Aside from occasional trips, he writes in his room until moving to Boston in 1836.

1828—Hawthorne pays Marsh and Capen of Boston one hundred dollars to publish his first novel, *Fanshawe*. Hawthorne later destroys every copy he can, urging his friends and relatives to do the same. Hawthorne later reported burning many of his early tales and sketches.

1830—Tales and biographical sketches by Hawthorne appear in *The Token* and *The Salem Gazette*. This work reveals Hawthorne's study of colonial history, an enterprise inspired partly by his interest in his ancestor, John Hawthorne (1641–1717), a magistrate in the Salem witch trials. Although Hawthorne assembles collections of tales, he can publish only individual short stories and sketches until 1837.

1836—Hawthorne moves to Boston to edit *The American Magazine of Useful and Entertaining Knowledge*. With his sister Elizabeth, he also edits *Peter Parley's Universal History on the Basis of Geography*.

March 1837—*Twice-Told Tales* is published by the American Stationers' Company of Boston in an edition of one thousand. Without Hawthorne's knowledge, Horatio Bridge guarantees $250 to ensure the book's publication.

November 1837—Hawthorne meets Sophia Peabody, whom he later marries.

16 January 1839—Hawthorne begins work as an inspector in the Boston Custom-House. It was the first of many jobs Hawthorne would take, and, as always, he found it impossible to write. He works here until January 1841.

November 1840—Hawthorne publishes *Grandfather's Chair*, a children's book, soon followed by two others: *Famous Old People* and *Liberty Tree*.

12 April 1841—Hawthorne joins the community at Brook Farm, hoping he and Sophia can live there after their marriage. He becomes a trustee, one of three directors of finance, and contributes finan-

cially to the community, but cannot write there. He leaves in November 1841.

1842—The second Edition of *Twice-Told Tales* appears. On 9 July, he marries Sophia, settles in the Old Manse and writes regularly. On 3 March 1844, their first child, Una, is born.

October 1845—Because of financial difficulties, Hawthorne and his family to move in with his mother and sisters in Salem until March. In April, Hawthorne begins work as surveyor at the Salem Custom-house.

22 July 1846—Hawthorne's son Julian is born, and his short story collection *Mosses from an Old Manse* is published.

7 June 1849—Hawthorne loses his job at the Custom-house. His mother dies in July, and in August, he begins writing *The Scarlet Letter*, published in March 1850.

May 1850—The Hawthornes move to Lenox, Massachusetts. In August, Hawthorne meets Herman Melville, who dedicates *Moby-Dick* to Hawthorne the following year. Hawthorne begins writing *The House of the Seven Gables*, which appears early in 1851. 20 May 1851, his second daughter, Rose Hawthorne, is born. Late in 1851, *The Snow Image and Other Twice-Told Tales* is published. A new edition of *Twice-Told Tales* also appears in 1851. Hawthorne starts writing *A Wonder-Book for Girls and Boys*, adaptations of classical myths for children, and *The Blithedale Romance*, both published in 1852.

June 1852—The Hawthornes move to The Wayside in Concord. 27 July 1852, Hawthorne's sister Louisa dies in a fire as she travels by boat to visit him. By the end of August, he completes the *Life of Franklin Pierce*, a campaign biography of his close friend who is elected president of the United States in November.

1853—Hawthorne publishes *Tanglewood Tales*, more classical myths for children.

July 1853—The Hawthornes sail for Liverpool, where Hawthorne will serve as counsel until his resignation on 31 August 1857. He is unable to escape these duties until 5 January 1858, when Hawthorne and his family leave for France, then Italy, where they remain until their return to England on 24 June 1859.

1854—The second edition of *Mosses from an Old Manse* appears.

1860—*The Marble Faun* is published, and the Hawthornes return to the Wayside.

1863—*Our Old Home*, a collection of sketches about England, is published.

19 May 1864—Hawthorne dies.

Source: Arlin Turner, *Nathaniel Hawthorne: A Biography* (New York: Oxford University Press, 1980).

Selected Bibliography

Primary Sources

Most of Hawthorne's writings are collected in a scholarly edition: *The Centenary Edition of the Works of Nathaniel Hawthorne*, 20 vols. edited by William Charvat, Roy Harvey Pearce, Claude M. Simpson, Thomas Woodson, Matthew Bruccoli, Fredson Bowers, Bill Ellis, James Rubino, J. Donald Crowley, L. Neal Smith, James Kayes, John Manning, Edward H. Davidson, and Norman Holmes Pearson. Columbus, Ohio: Ohio State University Press, 1962–1988. This collection is identified below as *The Centenary Edition*. Also, the number in parenthesis after the title of the work is the date of first publication.

Short Fiction Collections

Mosses from an Old Manse (1846, 2d. ed. 1854). *The Centenary Edition*, Volume X.
"The Old Manse," "The Birth-mark" (1843), "A Select Party" (1844), "Young Goodman Brown" (1835), "Rappaccini's Daughter" (1844), "Mrs. Bullfrog" (1837), "Fire Worship" (1843), "Buds and Bird-Voices" (1843), "Monsieur du Miroir" (1837), "The Hall of Fantasy" (1843), "The Celestial Rail-road" (1843), "The Procession of Life" (1843), "Feathertop" (1852, collected in 1854), "The New Adam and Eve" (1843), "Egotism; or, The Bosom Serpent" (1843), "The Christmas Banquet" (1844), "Drowne's Wooden Image" (1844), "The Intelligence Office" (1844), "Roger Malvin's Burial" (1832), "P.'s Correspondence" (1845), "Earth's Holocaust" (1844), "Passages from a Relinquished Work" (1834, collected in 1854), "Sketches from Memory" (1835, collected in 1854), "The Old Apple-Dealer" (1843), "The Artist of the Beautiful" (1844), "A Virtuoso's Collection" (1842).

The Snow Image (1851). *The Centenary Edition*, Volume XI.
"Preface" (1852), "The Snow-Image" (1851), "The Great Stone Face" (1850), "Main-street" (1849), "Ethan Brand" (1850), "A Bell's Biography" (1837), "Sylph Etherege" (1838), "The Canterbury Pilgrims" (1833), "Old News" (1835), "The Man of Adamant" (1837), "The Devil in Manuscript" (1835), "John Inglefield's Thanksgiving" (1840), "Old Ticonderoga" (1836), "The Wives of the Dead" (1832), "Little Daffydowndilly" (1843), "My Kinsman, Major Molineux" (1832).

Twice-Told Tales (1837, eds. 1842, 1851–1853). *The Centenary Edition*, Volume IX.

"Preface" (1851), "The Gray Champion" (1835), "Sunday at Home" (1837), "The Wedding Knell" (1836), "The Minister's Black Veil" (1836), "The May-pole of Merry Mount" (1836), "The Gentle Boy" (1832), "Mr. Higginbotham's Catastrophe" (1834), "Little Annie's Ramble" (1835), "Wakefield" (1835), "A Rill from the Town Pump" (1835), "The Great Carbuncle" (1837), "The Prophetic Pictures" (1837), "David Swan" (1837), "Sights from a Steeple" (1831), "The Hollow of the Three Hills" (1830), "The Toll-Gatherer's Day" (1837, collected in 1842), "The Vision of the Fountain" (1835), "Fancy's Show Box" (1837), "Dr. Heidegger's Experiment" (1837), "Howe's Masquerade" (1838, collected in 1842), "Edward Randolph's Portrait" (1838, collected in 1842), "Lady Eleanore's Mantle" (1838, collected in 1842), "Old Esther Dudley" (1839, collected in 1842), "The Haunted Mind" (1835, collected in 1842), "The Village Uncle" (1835, collected in 1842), "The Ambitious Guest" (1835, collected in 1842), "The Sister Years" (1839, collected in 1842), "Snow-flakes" (1838, collected in 1842), "The Seven Vagabonds" (1833, collected in 1842), "The White Old Maid" (1835, collected in 1842), "Peter Goldthwaite's Treasure" (1838, collected in 1842), "Chippings with a Chisel" (1838, collected in 1842), "The Shaker Bridal" (1838, collected in 1842), "Night Sketches" (1838, collected in 1842), "Endicott and the Red Cross" (1838, collected in 1842), "The Lily's Quest" (1839, collected in 1842), "Footprints on the Sea-shore" (1838, collected in 1842), "Edward Fane's Rosebud" (1837, collected in 1842), "The Threefold Destiny" (1838, collected in 1842).

Uncollected Short Fiction

The Centenary Edition, Volume XI.

"Alice Doane's Appeal." *The Token and Atlantic Souvenir*. Boston: Charles Bowen, 1835. 84–101.

"The Antique Ring." *Sargent's New Monthly Magazine of Literature, Fashion, and the Fine Arts* 1 (February 1842): 80–86.

"The Battle-Omen." *Salem Gazette* 44, n.s. 8 (2 November 1830): 1.

"A Book of Autographs." *United States Magazine and Democratic Review* 15 (November 1844): 454–461.

"Fragments from the Journal of a Solitary Man." *Atlantic Monthly* 10 (July 1837): 45–56.

"The Ghost of Doctor Harris," *The Nineteenth Century* 47 (January 1900): 88–93.

"A Good Man's Miracle," *Child's Friend* 1 (February, 1844): 151–156.

"Graves and Goblins." *New England Magazine* 8 (June 1835): 438–444.

"My Visit to Niagara." *New England Magazine* 8 (February 1835): 91–96.

"An Old Woman's Tale." *Salem Gazette* 44, n.s. 8 (December 21, 1830): 1–2.

"Sketches from Memory." *New England Magazine* 9 (December 1935): 404–409.

"Time's Portraiture." *Salem Gazette*, broadside, 1 January 1838.

"A Visit to the Clerk of the Weather." *American Monthly* 7 (May 1836): 483–487.

Novels

The Blithdale Romance (1852). *The Centenary Edition*, Volume 3.
Fanshawe (1828). *The Centenary Edition*, Volume 3.
The House of the Seven Gables (1851). *The Centenary Edition*, Volume 2.
The Marble Faun (1860). *The Centenary Edition*, Volume 4.
The Scarlet Letter (1850). *The Centenary Edition*, Volume 1.

Nonfiction

The American Notebooks (1868). *The Centenary Edition*, Volume 8.
The French and Italian Notebooks (1871). *The Centenary Edition*, Volume 14.
Hawthorne as Editor, edited by Arlin Turner. University, Louisiana: Louisiana State University Press, 1941.
Hawthorne's Lost Notebook, transcribed by Barbara S. Mouffe. University Park, Pennsylvania: Penn State University Press, 1978.
The Letters 1813–1843. The Centenary Edition, Volume 15.
The Letters 1843–1853. The Centenary Edition, Volume 16.
The Letters 1853–1856. The Centenary Edition, Volume 17.
The Letters 1857–1864. The Centenary Edition, Volume 18.
The Letters 1853–1855. The Centenary Edition, Volume 19.
The Letters 1856–1857. The Centenary Edition, Volume 20.
Life of Franklin Pierce. Boston: Ticknor, Reed, and Fields, 1852.
Miscellanies: Biographical and other Sketches and Letters. The Writings of Nathaniel Hawthorne, Volume 17. Boston and New York: Houghton, Mifflin and Company, 1900.
Our Old Home: A Series of English Sketches (1863).*The Centenary Edition*, Volume 5.

Children's Books

Tanglewood Tales (1853). *Centenary Edition*, Volume 7.
True Stories from History and Biography (1852). *Centenary Edition*, Volume 6.
Twenty Days with Julian and Little Bunny. Privately published by S. H. Wakeman, 1904.
A Wonder Book (1851). *Centenary Edition*, Volume 7.

Unfinished Manuscripts

The American Claimant Manuscripts. The Centenary Edition, Volume 12.
    "The Ancestral Footstep (1882–83), " "Etherege," "Grimshawe."
The Elixir of Life Manuscripts. The Centenary Edition, Volume 13.
    Septimus Felton (1872), "Septimus Norton," *The Dolliver Romance* (1876).

Sources: *The Centenary Edition.*
  C. E. Frazer Clark, Jr. *Nathaniel Hawthorne: A Descriptive Bibliography.* Pittsburgh, Pennsylvania: University of Pittsburgh Press, 1978.

Secondary Sources

Books and Parts of Books

Baym, Nina. *The Shape of Hawthorne's Career.* Ithaca: Cornell University Press, 1976.

————. "Thwarted Nature: Nathaniel Hawthorne as Feminist," in *American Novelists Revisited: Essays in Feminist Criticism.* Ed. Fritz Fleischmann. Boston: G. K. Hall, 1982. 58–77.

Becker, Isidore H. *The Ironic Dimension in Hawthorne's Short Fiction.* New York: Carlton Press, 1971.

Bell, Millicent. *Hawthorne's View of the Artist.* Albany, New York: University of New York Press, 1962.

Bensick, Carol Marie. *La Nouvelle Beatrice: Renaissance and Romance in "Rappaccini's Daughter."* New Brunswick, New Jersey: Rutgers University Press, 1985.

Borges, Jorge Luis. *Other Inquisitions: 1937–1952.* Trans. Ruth L. C. Simms. Austin, Texas: University of Texas Press, 1964. 47–65.

Brodhead, Richard. *The School of Hawthorne.* New York: Oxford University Press, 1986.

Chandler, Elizabeth Lathrop. *A Study of the Sources of the Tales and Romances Written by Nathaniel Hawthorne before 1853.* Darby, Pennsylvania: Arden Library, 1978.

Colacurcio, Michael J. *The Province of Piety: Moral History in Hawthorne's Early Tales.* Cambridge, Massachusetts: Harvard University Press, 1984.

Crews, Frederick. *The Sins of the Fathers: Hawthorne's Psychological Themes.* New York: Oxford University Press, 1966.

Current-Garcia, Eugene. *The American Short Story before 1850: A Critical History.* Boston: G. K. Hall, 1985. 42–59, 151–56.

Doubleday, Neal F. *Hawthorne's Early Tales: A Critical Study.* Durham, North Carolina: Duke University Press, 1972.

Ehrlich, Gloria. *Family Themes and Hawthorne's Fiction: The Tenacious Web.* New Brunswick, New Jersey: Rutgers University Press, 1984.

Fick, Leonard J. *The Light Beyond: A Study of Hawthorne's Theology.* Westminster, Maryland: The Newman Press, 1955.

Fogle, Richard Harter. *Hawthorne's Fiction: The Light and the Dark.* Norman, Oklahoma: University of Oklahoma Press, 1964.

Folsom, James K. *Man's Accidents and God's Purposes: Multiplicity in Hawthorne's Fiction.* New Haven: College and University Press, 1963.

Gollin, Rita. *Nathaniel Hawthorne and the Truth of Dreams.* Baton Rouge, Louisiana: Louisiana State University Press, 1979.

Howells, William D. *Literary Friends and Acquaintance.* New York: Harper & Brothers Publishers, 1901. 49–57.

James, Henry. *Hawthorne.* New York: Harper & Brothers, 1879.

Johnson, Claudia. *The Productive Tension of Hawthorne's Art.* University, Alabama: University of Alabama Press, 1981.

Male, Roy R. *Hawthorne's Tragic Vision.* Austin, Texas: University of Texas Press, 1957.

Martin, Terence. *Nathaniel Hawthorne.* Boston: Twayne Publishers, 1983.

McPherson, Hugo. *Hawthorne as Myth-Maker: A Study in Imagination.* Toronto: University of Toronto Press, 1971.

Mellow, James R. *Nathaniel Hawthorne in His Times.* Boston: Houghton, Mifflin, 1980.

Pearce, Roy Harvey, *Hawthorne Centenary Essays.* Columbus, Ohio: Ohio State University Press, 1964.

Rohrberger, Mary. *Hawthorne and the Modern Short Story: A Study in Genre.* The Hague: Mouton & Company, 1966.

Schubert, Leland. *Hawthorne, the Artist: Fine-Art Devices in Fiction.* Chapel Hill: The University of North Carolina Press, 1944.

Stein, William Bysshe. *Hawthorne's Faust, a Study of the Devil Archetype.* Gainesville: University of Florida Press, 1953.

Stewart, Randall. *Nathaniel Hawthorne: A Biography.* New Haven: Yale University Press, 1948.

Taylor, J. Golden. *Hawthorne's Ambivalence Toward Puritanism.* Logan, Utah: Utah State University Press, 1965.

Turner, Arlin. *Nathaniel Hawthorne: A Biography.* New York: Oxford University Press, 1980.

Articles and Reviews

Abel, Darrel. "Black Glove and Pink Ribbon: Hawthorne's Metonymic Symbols." *New England Quarterly* 42 (1969) : 163–180.

———. "The Theme of Isolation in Hawthorne." *Personalist* 32 (January and April 1951) : 42–59, 182–190.

Adams, Richard P. "Hawthorne: The Old Manse Period." *Tulane Studies in English* 8 (1958) : 115–151.

———. "Hawthorne's *Provincial Tales.*" *New England Quarterly* 30 (March 1957) : 39–57.

Askew, Melvin W. "Hawthorne, The Fall, and The Psychology of Maturity." *American Literature* 34 (November 1962) : 335–343.

Browne, Ray B. "The Oft-Told *Twice Told Tales*: Their Folklore Motifs." *Southern Folklore Quarterly* 22 (June 1958) : 69–85.

Selected Bibliography

Longfellow, Henry Wadsworth. *"Twice-Told Tales." North American Review* 54 (April 1842) : 496–499.
McDonald, John J. " 'The Old Manse' and Its Mosses." *Texas Studies in Literature and Language* 16 (1974) : 77–108.
————. "The Old Manse Period Canon." *Nathaniel Hawthorne Journal* 2 (1972) : 13–39.
Melville, Herman. "Hawthorne and his *Mosses* By A Virginian Spending July in Vermont." *Literary World* 7 (17 and 24 August 1850) : 125–127, 145–147.
Poe, Edgar A. "Tale Writing: Mr. Hawthorne." *Godey's Lady's Book* 35 (November 1847) : 252–256.
Ringe, Donald A. "Hawthorne's Psychology of Head and Heart." *Publications of the Modern Language Association* 65 (March 1950) : 120–132.
Trollope, Anthony. "The Genius of Nathaniel Hawthorne." *North American Review* 129 (1879) : 203–222.
Warren, Robert Penn. "Hawthorne Revisited: Some Remarks on Hellfiredness." *Sewanee Review* 81 (1973) : 75–111.

Bibliographies

Boswell, Jeanetta. *Nathaniel Hawthorne and the Critics: A Checklist of Criticism 1900–1978.* Metuchen, N. J.: The Scarecrow Press, Inc, 1982.
Clark, C. E. Frazer. *Nathaniel Hawthorne: A Descriptive Bibliography.* Pittsburgh: University of Pittsburgh Press, 1978.
Jones, Buford. *A Checklist of Hawthorne Criticism, 1951–1966.* Hartford, Connecticut: Transcendental Books, 1967.
Newman, Lea Bertini Vozar. *A Reader's Guide to the Short Stories of Nathaniel Hawthorne.* Boston: G. K. Hall, 1979.

Index

"Artist of the Beautiful, The," *36–38*, 47, 136; criticism of, 36, 140, 146–49

"Birth-mark, The," 4, *28–30*, 34, 85, 136; criticism of, 131, 134, 137, 139, 140

"Bosom Serpent, The"; *see* "Egotism; or, the Bosom Serpent"

"Celestial Rail-road, The," *61–62*, 64

"Chippings with a Chisel," 43–48

"Christmas Banquet, The," 129

"Custom-House, The" (*The Scarlet Letter*), *117–19*, 133

"Dr. Heidegger's Experiment," *33–36*, 136; criticism of, 34, 131

"Drowne's Wooden Image," *48–51*, 52, 54, 55, 76, 136

"Earth's Holocaust," *24–25*, 128

"Egotism; or, the Bosom Serpent," *22–24*, 129, 136; criticism of, 131

"Endicott and the Red Cross," 136

"Ethan Brand," *30–33*, 35, 55, 136; criticism of, 31, 32

"Great Carbuncle, The," *73–75*, 136; criticism of, 74, 131

"Great Stone Face, The," *75–77*, 85; criticism of, 77

"Hall of Fantasy, The," 55–58

"Haunted Mind, The," 78–79

"Hollow of the Three Hills, The," 136

"Intelligence Office," 129

"Lady Eleanore's Mantle," *17–18*, 20, 22

"Legends of the Province-House, The," 136

"Little Annie's Ramble," 70, 130

"Man of Adamant, The," *20–22*, 23; criticism of, 20, 138

"May-pole of Merry Mount, The," *72–73*, 136; criticism of, 73

"Minister's Black Veil, The," *18–20*, 22, 136; criticism of, 135, 137

"Monsieur du Miroir," 128

"My Kinsman, Major Molineux," *6–11*, 136; criticism of, 10–11

"New Adam and Eve, The," 69–70

"Old News," 58–61

"Prophetic Pictures, The," *41–43*, 47, 136; criticism of, 42, 43

"Rappaccini's Daughter," 3, *67–71*, 136; criticism of, 69, 71, 131, 137, 139, 140

"Rill from the Town Pump, A," 71, 90

"Roger Malvin's Burial," *14–16*, 21, 136, 143, 145n5; criticism of, 136, 137, 138, 143, 144; *see also* "Lovewell's Fight"

"Shaker Bridal, The," criticism of, 136–37; 138

"Sights from a Steeple," 62–65

"Snow-Image, The," 5, *51–55*, 76, 136; criticism of, 131

The Author

Nancy Bunge is a professor in the Department of American Thought and Language at Michigan State University. She received her A.B. in philosophy from Radcliffe College, her M.A. in English literature from the University of Chicago, and her Ph.D. in American literature from the University of Wisconsin at Madison. She has published literary analyses of nineteenth- and twentieth-century American writers in journals including *The Nathaniel Hawthorne Journal, Studies in Short Fiction*, and *The Walt Whitman Review*. She has also published interviews with contemporary poets and fiction writers in *The American Poetry Review* and *The Washington Post*. Sixteen of her interviews are collected in *Finding the Words: Conversations with Writers Who Teach* (Swallow Press/Ohio University Press, 1985). She was a senior Fulbright lecturer in American literature and culture at the University of Vienna.

The Editor

General Editor Gordon Weaver earned his B.A. in English at the University of Wisconsin-Milwaukee in 1961; his M.A. in English at the University of Illinois, where he studied as a Woodrow Wilson Fellow, in 1962; and his Ph.D. in English and creative writing at the University of Denver in 1970. He is author of several novels, including *Count a Lonely Cadence, Give Him a Stone, Circling Byzantium*, and most recently *The Eight Corners of the World* (1988). Many of his numerous short stories are collected in *The Entombed Man of Thule, Such Waltzing Was Not Easy, Getting Serious, Morality Play, A World Quite Round*, and *Men Who Would Be Good* (1991). Recognition of his fiction includes the St. Lawrence Award for Fiction (1973), two National Endowment for the Arts Fellowships (1974, 1989), and the O. Henry First Prize (1979). He edited *The American Short Story, 1945–1980: A Critical History*, and is currently editor of *Cimarron Review*. He is professor of English at Oklahoma State University. Married, and the father of three daughters, he lives in Stillwater, Oklahoma.